After Life

My Journey
from
Incarceration
to Freedom

Alice Marie Johnson

with Nancy French

HARPER

An Imprint of HarperCollins*Publishers*

HarperCollins books may be purchased for educational, business, or sales promotional use. For information, please email the Special Markets Department at SPsales@harpercollins.com.

FIRST EDITION

Designed by William Ruoto

Library of Congress Cataloging-in-Publication Data has been applied for.

ISBN 978-0-06-293610-3

19 20 21 22 23   LSC   10 9 8 7 6 5 4 3 2 1

To my parents, Raymond and Sallie Mae Boggan,
who gave me a strong foundation of faith and never stopped
praying for me and believing that I would one day be free.

Foreword

—◠—

"This is so unfair."

On the evening on October 25, 2017, I was scrolling through Twitter when I came across a video that changed my life. Someone I follow had retweeted a video telling the story of Alice Marie Johnson. I had never heard Alice's name before that day, but the heading caught my attention. A sixty-two-year-old great-grandmother had been in prison for twenty-one years for a first-time, nonviolent drug offense. How is that possible?

I watched as Miss Alice told the story of how her desperation, after losing her job and struggling to put food on the table for her children, led her to make a bad decision that resulted in her being sentenced to life in prison without the possibility of parole. My immediate reaction was to tweet how I felt. *This is so unfair.*

"The real Miss Alice is a woman who has made a mistake." I felt completely heartbroken for Alice. I could see how much she loved her family, and how much pain and loss she had experienced being away from them for so long. I couldn't imagine being without mine. But there was something about her outlook that inspired me. The way she talked about love, hope, and regret. Alice had this incredible pride in having been able to mentor women in prison to help them cope with doing their time behind bars. I knew I had to help her get out from behind hers.

That night I couldn't stop thinking about Alice. Her story haunted me. Imagine spending two decades in a prison cell, away from family and friends, watching life pass you by out of a window that never opens. Knowing that no matter how much you accomplish on the inside, or how well you behave, you're never getting out. That was Alice's life. She had missed the birth of her grandkids and her parents had both passed away while she was in prison. Life was beginning and ending as she sat behind bars because of one terrible mistake.

For years I've had a fascination with true crime. I've seen every crime documentary out there. *Making a Murderer, The Staircase, The Jinx*, you name it, I've seen it. But nothing had impacted me as much as that four-minute-long video about Miss Alice. I was feeling angry about her situation, sad about the life that was taken away from her, and disappointed in our justice system. I decided to reach out to my friend Shawn Holley, who had worked on the OJ case with my dad back in 1995. I had an odd obsession with true crime but I had no real experience with the legal system and no idea if there was anything I could do to help Alice, but I just knew I had to try. I texted Shawn that night to learn more about Alice's situation and what could be done. I wanted to understand our options. Shawn quickly found Alice's attorney and started to form a relationship.

I then decided to reach out to Ivanka Trump. I had known Ivanka and her family for years and I felt that Ivanka would have compassion, as a woman and as a mom, and would understand how important this was. Ivanka listened to everything I had to say and felt the same way I did. She connected me with her husband, Jared Kushner, who was passionate about criminal justice reform and believed in Alice's case.

There was only one way to get Alice out of prison. She had to be granted clemency, which meant I had to go directly to the only person who has the power to grant Alice the second chance she deserved: the president. And I had to be prepared. It took about six months to get all of Alice's files together and we waited patiently to be given a date when we could visit the White House to meet with President Trump and tell Alice's story. When we finally got a date, it ended up being rescheduled, and the new date fell on Alice's birthday. I felt like this had to be a good sign. This was Alice's day; she was all that mattered and I wasn't going to let her down.

The day arrived, and as we sat in the Oval Office with the president and told him Alice's story, I felt empowered by the atmosphere in this room. It's an amazing feeling to sit in a place that has so much history, where momentous decisions are made that impact an entire nation. If it's possible to feel both overwhelmed and serene at the same time, that's how I felt. An overwhelming sense of serenity, I guess you could say. I was exactly where I was meant to be, in that place, at that time. I left the White House feeling happy and hopeful.

I wasn't told how long it would take before as decision would be made, just that I would get a call from the president when the time came. About a week later I was at a photoshoot in New York when I got the call. I held my breath as President Trump told me his decision. He was granting her clemency. Miss Alice was going home.

But the best moment was yet to come. I got on a call right away with the attorneys and they called the prison to connect Alice to the call. I assumed that Alice's attorneys had given her the good news before I joined the call, but when she picked up the phone I could tell by the sound of her voice that she didn't know yet. Twenty-one years, and I wasn't going to let her spend another second in that cell. "We did it, Alice. You're out." On the other end, I heard Alice scream. The sound of joy, amazement, relief, hope, grace, all at once. That moment will forever be one of my favorite memories.

Alice's story has inspired me more than I ever thought possible. Too often we are discouraged because we think something will be too challenging, or that an idea is too crazy, or the chance of success too rare. Miss Alice found herself in a position where most of us would have felt completely hopeless. But in spite of it all, she stayed positive, used her time to support others, and most important, never gave up hope. I took that with me throughout my journey to free Alice, and I take that with me every day, with everything I do.

Thank you, Miss Alice, my dear friend, my inspiration, my family. You have helped me find an incredible new sense of purpose, and I am so grateful for that. You have helped create change that will impact others, and have inspired and encouraged me to continue on my journey to do the same.

—Kim Kardashian West

Chapter 1

⌒

I sat up in my bunk at Federal Medical Center, Carswell, a prison in Texas. It was a Saturday, and we still had an hour or two before we had to stand in our cell to be officially counted by the guards. There were two bunks in each overcrowded cell, housing four women in a space designed for two. I left my bunk area and walked down to my friend's cell.

"Josette," I whispered at the door. We weren't allowed to walk into each other's cells, and I didn't want to disturb her roommate. "I need to talk to you. Can you step out here?"

She looked up from her bunk, which she was making up. Instead of finishing, she turned and put on her slippers and came to me. We frequently walked through the atrium together, on the way to the microwave or just to stretch our legs. She and her sister Tracey were in prison, but I never pried about how they ended up there. It's rude to ask people about their crimes, and I never wanted my impression of them to change based on their past. I took them as they were in that second, on that day.

I had to live in the moment. After all, I couldn't change the past, and the future would always be the same as this day, yesterday, and the day before that.

In 1996, after a series of bad decisions resulted in my desperate (and illegal) attempt to make money, I was sentenced to life for my role in a Memphis drug conspiracy. I'd been told I wouldn't leave prison unless I was carried out as a corpse.

But part of me didn't believe it.

"What's wrong?" Josette asked, her brow furrowed.

"I had another dream."

"Let me guess," she said. "You got released again?"

Okay, so maybe being freed is a normal fantasy for people serving life sentences, but my dreams had taken on an important role while I was in prison.

"This one was so real I couldn't get it out of my head," I said.

Josette came out of her cell, and this time we didn't walk across the shiny cement floors of the atrium together. I didn't want to be interrupted by the stares of other prisoners.

"I dreamed the case manager called me down to the office and said, 'I have a phone call for you.' When I got on the phone, I heard the voice of a woman. She said, 'Alice, you're being released from prison!'"

Josette's eyes widened.

"I know I'm going to walk out of here," I told her.

"I believe you," she said earnestly. "But was that the whole dream?"

I felt like I was reliving it as I described it. I tilted my head and told her the rest of it more slowly.

"I didn't even take the time to get all of my belongings, I just went outside. And there were many reporters putting microphones in front of my mouth. The microphones had the network logos emblazoned on them." When I told Josette this detail, she laughed. Over the years, many women in the prison had come up to me and said, "I had a crazy dream about you, Miss Alice." It didn't matter if they were white, black, or Hispanic, the dreams all had the same theme: I was released and the media was reporting on it.

"But this is the confusing part," I said. Josette stood in rapt attention. "A beautiful woman was responsible for getting me out of prison. In the dream, I could see her face, and she was so very pretty."

"Who could that have been?" Josette asked. "Your daughter?"

"Maybe. Who else would care enough to try to get me out of here?" I asked. "I only know she was beautiful, but I didn't recognize her."

Chapter 2

On May 30, 1955, Raymond Boggan sent for the midwife, Miss Hannah, as his wife's labor pains came closer and closer together. When Miss Hannah arrived and checked on Sallie Mae, she came out of the room with a smile on her face.

"That baby is coming, but not until tomorrow," she announced, speaking with the confidence that came from ushering dozens of babies into the world. "I'll be back first thing in the morning."

But before she could open the front door to leave, a baby's loud scream echoed throughout the house. My mother would later tell me that it looked like I had stood up and propelled myself out. My time had come. I had arrived.

By the time my parents were done, they had nine children. In order from oldest to youngest, they were Lena, Celestine, Coria, Thelma, Julius, me, Patricia, Ruby, and Dolores. Eight girls and one boy. Seemed liked Mama was always having babies, a process that fascinated me.

All of us but Patricia were born at home. When the doctors/ midwives showed up at the house to help deliver them, they'd take their black leather bag into the bedroom. After a while, I'd hear a baby cry and they'd come out with yet another little sister. For years, I was absolutely sure babies came out of those black medical bags, a biological certainty I'd tell everyone I knew. No one ever corrected me. People assumed you were acting too grown if you tried to find out more about such topics.

Along with some other family members, fourteen of us lived in a small cinder block house a landowner named Mr. Abernathy provided in Cockrum, Mississippi. The house had two bedrooms, a living room, and a kitchen, though we had no running water. We had an outhouse, where we used newspapers instead of toilet paper. In one bedroom, we had two big beds, three in each bed vertically, and a couple at the bottom of the bed horizontally. I hated sleeping at the foot of the bed, because I disliked waking up with feet in my face. No matter where I was situated, however, I couldn't toss or turn. We fit snugly together and dared not move until the next day, when the sun's rays came through the poorly insulated windows and warmed us.

Mr. Abernathy allowed my parents to farm his land in exchange for a share of the crop. He got a really good deal, since my daddy, Raymond, and my mama, Sallie Mae, had lots of children to help farm. Since Mama was busy having babies, most of the work done on the farm was done by Daddy and us kids.

"This is the last time we'll have to work these cotton fields," my daddy told us at the beginning of every year. We had family in Gary, Indiana, who promised us that if we ever could make it up north, they'd help my daddy get a job in the steel industry.

Until then, we had to chop cotton, which meant we went out into the cotton fields with a hoe and got all the weeds and the grass away from the cotton plants to give them room to grow. That work, done under the scorching Mississippi sun, earned us $3 per day. Then, in late August, the cotton popped out of its green shell, which turned into a dry, brown husk. The cotton caused the beautiful fields to look like snow. When I was five years old, Mama dressed me in long sleeves to protect my skin from the sun's rays and sent me out to do the repetitive, painful work. The edges of cotton bolls were prickly and sharp, so when I put my hand inside the boll and pulled the cotton out it'd scratch up my hands. We worked from sunup to sundown and would always beat my daddy out into the field, since he had to get up even earlier to milk the cows. He'd meet us out in the fields after milking, would pick cotton during the day, and then milk the cows again in the evening. My older sisters gave me a little sack to fill with cotton, but I probably didn't even get enough to make a Q-tip. But I did get faster. My sister Celestine—who had hands quicker than lightning—would pick three hundred pounds on her best days. We got paid two cents per pound. Once we were done with our fields, I remember my mama would send Julius and me to our aunts' house to help our cousins with their fields.

We made the most of it, though.

"Soon I will be done," my daddy would begin to sing during the long, monotonous days. Then we kids would join in. "With the troubles of the world . . . I'm going home to live with God." I joined in too—though my voice wasn't as smooth as my sisters'—and passed the time. "No more weepin' and wailin' . . . No more weepin' and wailin' . . . No more weepin' and wailin' . . ."

We always sang one song called "This May Be My Last Time," and my siblings would laugh because I couldn't pronounce my *L*s correctly.

"Come on, Marie," they'd egg me on, calling me by my middle name. "Sing it loud." I sang it sincerely, though it sounded like I was saying the word "ass" instead of "last." I didn't know why they were laughing, but I sang it loud. Regardless, the old spirituals kept us going hour after hour. Honestly, when I think back to those days, I remember those harmonies and that laughter more than any ache in my back or scratch on my hands.

No matter how much we picked, old man Abernathy kept the books. At the end of the season, he pasted a disappointed look on his face and told Daddy the cotton hadn't yielded as much as he needed. "Plus, you still owe me for seeds," he'd bark. "There's not enough money left over to pay you."

Dejected, my daddy would tell us we'd have to stay for one more year. I began imagining Gary, Indiana, the way some people considered the land of Canaan: a city flowing with milk and honey. But we never saw Indiana.

The work never stopped. I graduated from my small cotton sack to one that was four feet long. Once children got older and good at filling these sacks to the brim, they were given sacks made of burlap that were nine feet long, and they'd drag them on the ground as they worked. One year we picked twenty-eight bales of cotton. We thought for sure that this would be the year we could get away from Mr. Abernathy's farm.

At the end of the season, however, that mean old man created new ways to keep us in his debt. My parents couldn't very well accuse him of lying, and they realized Mr. Abernathy would never release us from our so-called obligations.

They came up with a plan, one that involved food. My mother spent all day making various kinds of soul food like fried chicken, barbecue, ribs, homemade breads, and pies. Even to this day, if I close my eyes, I can still smell the sweet aroma of my mama's blackberry cobbler wafting through that tiny house. After she cooked, she loaded everything into our car and then drove to places the Abernathys would never go, like black baseball games. I'd sit by her side while she was cooking. "Marie," my mama would say to me, "you can't ever mention this to anyone." I was named after my aunt Alice. Instead of calling me Li'l Alice, they called me by my middle name, Marie.

When we got to the black parts of town, Mama and Daddy would open up the trunk and secretly sell every morsel. Sometimes our car—nicknamed Nellie Bell—would break down on the way back home, so we'd have to get out and push. But with every step, we were getting further and further away from the poverty of the cotton fields. Little by little, my parents squirreled away money. Mr. Abernathy never suspected that my parents were working all day for him and still had enough energy and productivity to make money in other ways. But that's exactly what they did.

Daddy secretly bought a house in Olive Branch, which was

about ten miles from where we lived. The house was basically just a frame, probably not even a thousand square feet. During the days, Daddy got up early, milked the cows, picked cotton, then milked the cows again. Then, at night, he sneaked away to hang the Sheetrock on that wooden frame. He installed the windows, put down the floors, and eventually my mother hung the curtains. Once the house was finished, my parents moved our belongings just a few things at a time in the car during the night, so the Abernathys wouldn't be any the wiser.

Once, in the middle of the night, I woke up with a hand over my mouth. My mother looked at me with wide eyes and a finger over her own mouth.

"Shhhhhhh . . ."

I tried to talk, but she wouldn't let me. She scooped me up into her arms and put me into Nellie Bell's back seat. My whole family was there, including cousins and my uncles. The car was in neutral, the headlights were off. In the darkness, I tried to ask questions—Where were we going? Why was it a secret?—but every time I tried to ask, someone would put a hand over my mouth.

The men pushed the car quietly down the driveway, the only sound the gravel crunching beneath the wheels. No one said a word, until we finally made it to a little store down the road. When we got there, they turned on the headlights and everyone cheered. With all the secrecy and covert planning, you would've thought we were slaves escaping the plantation. Mr. Abernathy never suspected a thing, and I never saw that old house again. Looking back, I realize how much courage it took for my parents to defy mean old Mr. Abernathy like that in the Jim Crow South, but they did it for us kids. For our futures.

Though Olive Branch was only ten miles down the road, it felt like a whole other world. My daddy got a job as a welder, which meant we had more money. My mama got a job cooking at the Lions Club, the Jaycees, and both the white and the black schools. Later, she worked at a country club as the head chef. Consequently, our family became well respected in the community, and, as an added bonus, Mama was able to bring home fine food to feed us. You can't ever feel poor when you are feasting on filet mignon, even if you're eating leftovers from the rich white folk. Eventually, in 1975, she fulfilled her dream of opening her own restaurant—Sallie's Kitchen Restaurant—so we always ate as well as anyone else. By then, her cooking skills were so renowned that she didn't even have to advertise.

The new house had three bedrooms, a living room, a dining room, and even a bathroom. At first, it didn't have running water, so Julius slept in the bathroom—and I was jealous of him because, as the only boy, he had all the privacy. Every time I bring this up—even to this day—Julius points out that sleeping in the bathroom wasn't as glamorous as I made it out to be. When we did get the bathroom hooked up to water, I was the first one in my class with an indoor toilet. If you ever wanted a shortcut to popularity back then, indoor plumbing was it. Thankfully, Daddy loved gadgets. We were the first ones to get a party line telephone and the first ones to get a color television, so our home was the place all our friends wanted to be. To this day, I don't know how Mama made room for us all, but we always had plenty of room, food, and love.

I knew about love, but I was woefully uneducated when it came to sex and anatomy—which meant their strategy was working, as far as my parents were concerned. Once, however, when I was a Girl Scout, my sisters and I somehow came across a magazine that had photographs of nudists. I'd never seen a naked man before, so my sisters and I were shocked at the images we secretly viewed far away from Mama's watchful gaze. I was shocked when I saw the private parts of a man in the photo. I'd never seen anything like it, but I wasn't going to let my sisters know that.

"What are those?" My sister Patricia pointed at the photograph.

I always needed to have an answer, whether or not I actually knew what I was talking about. "Those are eggs," I said. "And that's a bird."

"What?" She gasped. "Well, that's the ugliest bird I've ever seen."

And so we made do, trying to figure out this topic by ourselves. Children were supposed to do as they were told and not ask questions.

⬦⬦⬦⬦⬦⬦

One thing I never needed to question was my faith. I've always known the Lord. If my parents ever wondered where I was, they knew to find me lying down in the grass somewhere, looking up at the sky and talking to Jesus. I was ten years old when I wrote my first poem, called "Who Is He?"

It began:

Sometimes, I look upon the fields
At the scattered hay and blowing mills
And I wonder
Who made us all?
Was he big or was he tall?
Does he stand erect with pride?
Can he see my glistening eyes?
Can you hear his voice so clear?
When he is not even near?
Those things I cannot say
Because I wasn't there that glorious day.

When I recited that poem at school, my teacher called other teachers into the room to hear me say it. They entered me into a competition with the middle schoolers, and I won even though I was younger than the rest of the entrants.

Daddy was a praying man. When he prayed, the whole church lit up. Prayers were some of the only times I ever saw my daddy cry, he'd sometimes be so moved by the experience. When he walked into even a visiting church, they'd call him up to the front and say, "Mr. Boggan is here. Can you lead us in prayer or a song?" Mama was very encouraging, but if Daddy ever missed a word she would definitely let him know.

Mama was our church's welcome and announcement person and mistress of ceremonies for as long as I can remember. On our way to church, she'd write down the order of the events and what she needed to say. She didn't have to plan too much in advance, because she had a ready-made choir with just her own kids. Plus, she had a knack for knowing who could do what. One memorable Sunday, the piano player didn't show up, and we walked in to see her sitting on the piano bench. It looked like the spirit was moving her, but the sounds coming from the piano didn't necessarily match her enthusiasm. She never said no to an opportunity and was never afraid to fill in when needed.

At some point, however, our parents' faith was not enough. When we got old enough, we were expected to join the church and be baptized. But you couldn't just walk up to the preacher and tell him you wanted to join. Not back then. When I was eleven years old, my sister Patricia and I went down to the "mourner's bench," where the preacher approached us and motioned us to kneel during a weeklong revival.

Then the elders of the congregation gathered and sang songs really loudly all around us. They'd sing about driving "old Satan away," over and over. While they sang, we repeated, "Oh Lawd, save my soul, oh Lawd, save my soul."

We repeated this until the spirit hit us. How long that took, exactly, depended on the person and God . . . It usually took a week. Honestly, it would've embarrassed our parents if it took us too long, because people might have speculated we were full of sin. The congregation could tell when the Holy Spirit fell, when you started crying, running, shouting, or jumping for joy. That's when everyone knew God was there and that Satan had been driven out. I didn't stay too long. I came off the mourner's bench on Tuesday.

Maybe some people faked this enthusiasm for God, just to get on with the process, but not me. When I was on the mourner's bench, I focused on God and really felt His presence. When the spirit hit me, my shouting was purely exuberant praise. Afterward, I prepared to be baptized in the pond behind the church. I was dressed all in white and my gown was tied at the ankle so it wouldn't billow up in the water.

First, the deacons made sure there were no cows or snakes in the pond. Then three deacons and the preacher—all dressed in white too—waded out into the water. My daddy was a deacon, so he baptized me. Even though the water was muddy, I came up feeling fresh, clean, and oh so righteous.

Okay, so maybe I was just a little pious too. That was back when I knew everything.

Back then, parents didn't sit down and talk to their kids about serious issues. I learned all I ever needed to know about the important things in life by eavesdropping. We had one phone in the middle of the house. When my mama talked, she was like E. F. Hutton. All of us kids listened. When grown folks came over, my mama always shooed us kids away. But I never left. My favorite thing to do was to crouch just outside the room or behind a chair and listen to my parents talk about the world. This frequently included conversation about racial issues.

Amid all of the sad, depressing tales, they spoke hopefully about the future. It was during those times that I overheard my mother talking to her friends one day about a charismatic, peaceful man named Martin Luther King Jr. He seemed to give her so much courage, and I detected awe in her voice as she described him. I think he also inspired her to action. Mama was active with the NAACP so she could make sure black people voted for whomever they wanted. By helping the poor people in our Mississippi community, my mother was an unsung hero of the civil rights movement.

At the time, most places were segregated. Being educated in an all-black school meant we didn't think much about race. We had great black teachers, a talented black band, and we had some great achievers come out of little East Side High School. I loved to learn, and the Boggan kids had a reputation for being smart. Plus, I think people showed us special favor because of my mother, a woman truly ahead of her time. She cared about what would now be described as social justice issues, though at the time it just seemed like common courtesy, right and wrong.

When poor people—of either race—got into trouble, they called on Mama to help represent them in the courtroom. Usually, if she vouched for them, the judges would give more lenient sentences just based on her word. Or if people were being sentenced, they counted on her to show up at sentencing. The judge would allow her to essentially be the parole officer for that prisoner. She would promise to keep an eye on them, to make sure they were in church, and so forth. Also, she helped many people get their first jobs by speaking up for them. As a sign of just how well regarded they were, my mother and father were the first black grand marshals of the Olive Branch parade. Everyone in town knew about her cooking, which allowed her to get to know all the bankers and business owners. Because she treated everyone well, she and my father were very well regarded in the community by both whites and blacks alike.

But I just knew her as Mama. On Sunday mornings, she'd get up and make us breakfast—fried chicken, biscuits, gravy, and rice. We'd line up around the kitchen table, which had benches on either side of it, and my father would say the Lord's Prayer. (I could recite the Lord's Prayer before my ABCs.) Your age and rank in the family determined which piece of the chicken you got: the breast was for the most senior among us, and the youngest received the wing, which had less meat on the bone.

Mama got up early every Sunday morning and had both breakfast and dinner prepared before we'd head to Mount Gilliam Church in nearby Byhalia. Most of the time, she didn't invite people over for dinner, they just showed up. Our home was situated on a little hill, and people walking by could hear the music coming from our small house. They'd stop by to see what was going on and they'd stay for dinner. She always cooked more than enough to feed everyone. After we ate, my sister Celestine played spirituals on the piano and everyone sang. I danced next to the piano, perfectly free and full of joy.

Though we had next to nothing, we were richer than anyone I knew.

∞∞∞∞∞∞∞∞

One night, when I was tucked snugly in bed, I overheard grown-up conversation from the other room. My parents were talking to a man; I could tell that much from his deep voice. Though I strained to hear what they were saying, I couldn't make out the words. In the morning, he was gone.

This happened a few times. Then one night, my mama crept

into our room and woke us up, and I could hear that man's voice talking to my father. A stranger's voice.

"Y'all children, get up," she whispered. "I want you to meet somebody." We crawled out of bed and rubbed the sleep out of our eyes. I had been in a deep sleep and had no idea what time it was. We followed our mother to the living room. There, I saw a man who reminded me of my father sitting on the couch. He bore a strong resemblance to him—was he an uncle?—but I'd never seen him before. And so we sat, uncomfortably, in the room as my parents introduced us.

"This is Marie," my mama said, then went down the line introducing the rest of us. Though he was still, the man's eyes were full of emotion. When he looked at us adoringly, we felt like he was just drinking us in.

At the end of our short visit, he called us over to him. "Come here, baby," he said. "Do you know who I am?" Of course, it was a rhetorical question, since we'd never been introduced.

My brother later told me that this was our true grandfather. His name was Charlie Carter, but he went by Emmett Jones. He'd moved to Watson, Arkansas, and had created a life for himself. He was a woodsman—a logger—but he couldn't read. He got along fine without being able to read, but he'd fallen in love with a woman who lived in Milwaukee, Wisconsin. She wrote him love letters, full of sentiments he never would be able to enjoy. Instead of writing back, he kept the well-worn letters for years without knowing the content. When his factory offered him a promotion, he knew he couldn't perform the job without being literate. He turned the promotion down, but he was too proud to explain to his boss why.

He had a nice, secretive life in Arkansas, but he did have to go home for his mother's funeral. That's when the sheriff found out he was in town. When my grandfather discovered that the law was after him, he fled. He ran and jumped out the back door of the church to get away.

The man we called Uncle Dan was apparently my father's stepdad—not his biological dad. The true story, the one my parents couldn't trust us to know, was much darker. When my grandmother was pregnant with my father, our nighttime visitor had gone to buy some whiskey at a store owned by a white man. The man's daughter came out to the counter and started to flirt with him. The store owner came back to the counter, overheard the flirtatious banter, and pulled out a gun.

The man froze, but the store owner pulled the trigger anyway. Some of the buckshot struck the man, so he pulled out his pistol and returned fire. The store owner, hit, crumpled to the floor. Though the man didn't die, his self-defense altered the course of his life forever. He changed his name, ran away, and never stopped running from the law. He never got a chance to raise my father. This pained him very much, especially as time went on and he couldn't even know his grandchildren.

The only man I knew as my grandfather, the man we called Uncle Dan, married my grandmother even though she was pregnant with my dad, in order to give him a proper name and a future. Daddy looked legitimate, but everyone knew that he had been conceived by a different man—everyone but us grandkids. My real biological grandfather secretly visited us at night, for a few sleepy hours stretched out over years.

As a kid, I didn't realize how very tragic that actually was. But soon enough, I'd know the pain of family separation all too well.

Chapter 3

You are demonstrating that we can stick together. You are demonstrating that we are all tied in a single garment of destiny, and that if one black person suffers, if one black person is down, we are all down.

—Martin Luther King Jr.

"I don't want to say 'Yes, ma'am' to you anymore," I told my mama one afternoon.

That got her attention. We children never crossed our parents. Back then—at least in my family—kids obeyed their parents, and that was the end of the discussion. But my mother was intrigued more than anything else.

"And why is that, Marie?"

In the Jim Crow South, it was normal for black people to address white people by looking down as they said "Yes, ma'am," and "No, suh." Until I was five years old, I always heard my mama and daddy respond to the white Abernathys in this way, and I just hated the deference they had to show those people. When I explained this to my mom, her face softened. To my surprise, she agreed with me, and I've never said "Yes, ma'am" to anyone ever again.

As I grew up, I became known as someone who stood up for various causes. When my mother's brothers from Chicago visited, they were amazed at my fighting spirit. That's a polite way of saying I was buck wild.

"Watch this," my uncle said to another uncle. He pushed me down and I fell right into the dirt. His shove made me lose my breath, and I felt pain in my chest. Immediately I felt tears welling up inside my eyes, but I knew I was not going to give my uncles the satisfaction of knowing I'd been hurt. I jumped right back up.

"Look at this gal!" He hit me in my chest, and again I had to catch my breath. I jumped back up again. "Look how her shoulders are squared like she's going to hit back," one said, laughing. And so, they decided to teach me how to throw a punch, a skill they never showed any of my other siblings. "You might need this one day," they told me, as they taught me how to box. "But don't you tell Sallie Mae we taught you this." They even taught me how to arm wrestle. I did all sorts of crazy stuff that they taught me on the cool. But the biggest skill I learned through my interaction with my uncles was how to swallow back my tears.

I got a lot more popular when I took on two mean sisters at school who always double-teamed everyone—and I won. Thinking back on those days, I'm surprised these fights never made it into my public record, but I assume that's because my teachers respected my mother so much. Once I even fought for my brother in an epic battle that ended at our house.

Julius was in our neighborhood when some bullies started harassing one of our cousins. Since he was with his friends, he decided to stand up against them, but all his friends ran off. That meant Julius fought all five guys himself as long as he could, before returning home. The bullies followed him into our yard.

Big mistake.

We sisters saw the fight from the windows and could tell even from a distance that they'd really gotten Julius's eye good. Before they knew it, we all bailed out of our house with brooms and sticks like an army carrying swords and shields. I went out there and beat those boys using those fighting skills my uncles had taught me. We fought tooth and nail, until we heard the door to our house slam.

We all looked at the porch, only to see my normally quiet daddy standing there with a shotgun. He shot that gun into the air, and those bullies scattered like cockroaches. I learned the lesson right then and there: even if our friends abandoned us, my family stuck together in hard times.

Plus, I learned not to sit back and watch injustice occur.

Part of that injustice was how everyone was artificially separated by color. When we went to the doctor's office, there was a sign on the wall that showed which side was designated for colored people and which side was for the whites. Even after everything was supposed to be integrated, the sign stayed up and people stayed in their places.

Our town's dentist was notorious for watering down the pain

medication he gave to black patients. When I was nine years old, I needed to get a tooth pulled. I climbed into the seat, and he said, "Raise your hand if you can feel anything." He started digging around in my mouth, and I could feel every single horrible move. I raised my hand, but he kept digging. I raised it even higher, but he continued to ignore me.

Finally, the pain—of the tooth being pulled and of being ignored—was too great. So, instead of raising my hand as instructed, I lowered it, wrapped my hand around that dentist's balls, and twisted as hard as I could.

He jumped back and yelled in pain. Then he looked at me with contempt in his eyes and hissed, "Get this little n——er out of here and don't you ever bring her back in here again."

I was never allowed back, but it was worth it.

As the 1960s came to a close, this slow boil of the South's racial tensions—long a staple of our lives—became unavoidable. In February 1968, a malfunctioning garbage truck crushed two black Memphis garbage collectors to death, causing over a thousand black men from the Memphis Department of Public Works to go on strike. News of these deaths was passed from the lips of people in my community in hushed tones reserved for tragedies. The local branch of the NAACP, a group to which my mama belonged, passed a resolution supporting the strike. This made my house a central hub of concern, activism, and activity.

I didn't grow up hating white people. I guess that sounds odd in today's polarizing world, especially since we lived through sharecropping and Jim Crow. Because my mama was revered for her cooking by both black and white, my parents had friends of both colors. She taught me to respect all people and—above all else—to be filled with joy instead of bitterness. But even we couldn't escape the national racial tension simmering in the late 1960s, and we couldn't turn our heads at injustice.

My mama's friends dropped by at all hours to talk to her about how wrongly the sanitation workers were being treated. The following month, I heard Mama excitedly tell her friends that Martin Luther King Jr. himself had come to Memphis to stand in solidarity with the workers. Over 25,000 people gathered to hear him speak, the largest indoor gathering the civil rights movement had ever seen, and it was right there in my own backyard, across the Tennessee–Mississippi border. I didn't dare ask my mother if I could skip school, but you better believe that the message of Martin Luther King Jr. was felt throughout the area like an earthquake.

He promised to return to Memphis a few days later to lead a peaceful, nonviolent protest through the city. On the day of the scheduled protest, a large snowfall blanketed the city, which delayed his travel. However, on the rescheduled day—March 28— an estimated 22,000 students skipped school to demonstrate, and the crowds soon erupted into violence. Though the civil rights leaders tried to call off the demonstration, it was too late. Looters broke into downtown shops, and police shot and killed a sixteen-year-old boy. To make matters worse, police officers followed demonstrators into a church sanctuary, where they released tear gas and clubbed people as they writhed on the floor gasping for air. The mayor declared martial law, and four thousand National Guard troops flooded the city.

Normally, my mama didn't talk to us directly about these issues, but this was unavoidable. It was also important for us to
understand. She was so upset that she walked through the house
fussing over the state of our community. Now that we were older,
she entrusted us with more conversation, and we got to hear her
vent.

Dr. King almost didn't come back. He eventually decided that
it was important to come back to encourage Memphis to have a
nonviolent struggle for justice. His decision to return was controversial, and it turned out to be the one that ultimately ended his
life. As King was getting ready for dinner on April 4, just after
six o'clock, he was shot and killed on the balcony of the Lorraine
Motel.

I was almost thirteen. A collective wailing rippled throughout Memphis and the mid-South area. My parents cried as the
television news reporters talked about his assassination. My siblings and I found ourselves crying, not really realizing the mag-
nitude of what had just occurred. People came over to the house,
to grieve with my parents, and this time we were allowed to be in
the middle of the conversation. Everybody talking and grieving.

"What's going to become of us now?" wailed one of my parents' friends in the living room. Nothing seemed certain for black
people in America at the time. King was perceived as our libera-
tor, and his death was one of the most terrible events we had ever
experienced. A hopelessness settled on us. "What's going to happen next?" the friend continued. "Who's going to lead us?" In my
mind, a new civil war had broken out. On the news, I saw bombs

going off in the street. Violence. Looting. Tear gas. This was my community, and it was going up in flames.

In a way, I got radicalized during these tumultuous times. I even thought I wanted to join the Black Panthers, an idea I tossed out to my mother.

"If you quit school to become a Black Panther, you'll just be quitting school," she said. "There's no group to join. You better stop that crazy talk right now!" She was right, since we lived in rural Mississippi, so I'd have to go to Memphis to be a part of the revolution. Plus, my mama would never have gone for me quitting school anyway. I'd always been passionate about issues, but the seeds of activism took root in my heart after Dr. King was shot and killed.

Though King's death was a national tragedy, it felt personal to me.

When I was fourteen, I learned that a church leader was fooling around on the sly. During revival week, I couldn't bear looking at him standing in front of the congregation acting so godly in public but dancing with the devil in private. That sort of hypocrisy was too much for me.

I couldn't take it anymore. I jumped up and exclaimed, "There's more to God than this!" The people in the church got quiet and turned to looked at me. I caught my mama's eyes before I walked out the door. I made it to the parking lot before she caught up with me.

"What is wrong with you saying something like that?" she demanded.

I didn't answer.

She made me go back inside. In my family, church attendance was not optional. However, in my heart, I left organized religion that day.

When I walked away from the church, however, I ran right into the chaos of the culture. Things seemed to be spinning out of control. It had been a couple of years since Martin Luther King Jr. was assassinated, but the 1960s also brought us the sexual revolution, the Cuban missile crisis, the Vietnam War, the assassination of John F. Kennedy, the assassination of Robert Kennedy, riots at the Chicago Democratic National Convention, and a man on the moon. Things were changing, fluctuating, moving. I wanted to be a part of the revolution, something true.

In ninth grade, school administrators told us we'd be changing schools the following year. Desegregation. "Everything will be different," they told us. "Life is going to change." But things were already changing. My friends and I dressed modestly for school, but as soon as we got out of sight of our parents, we'd march straight to the bathroom and slip off our bras. We wore our modest pants or long skirts to get out of the house, but we slipped on miniskirts once we were out of our parents' sight. I even wore high heels to basketball games. I always looked older than I was. My older sister Thelma was always embarrassed by me, since the male fans of the visiting team—people who didn't know how young I was—always gave me more attention than I should've had.

I didn't burn any bras, but I certainly wanted to be free of society's restraints. The sexual revolution was gripping our nation, and Mississippi was not immune to its allure. I wanted to be a part of it. I wasn't even old enough to date, but my mama and daddy had been so busy trying to make a better life for us they'd gotten a little lax with me. Though they restricted the comings and goings of my other siblings, they regarded me differently from the other kids. I was older than my years indicated. At least, I seemed to be. It's almost as if they forgot I was only fourteen when I told them I wanted to date Charles, a guy in the band.

I played the French horn and the bells, and I was a concert oboist. Charles, who played the trumpet, loved to dance. On band trips, he and I had pushed the boundaries and danced with each other with abandon. He was two years older. I wish I could tell you some sweeping tale of high school sweethearts, our destinies intertwining forever. And, in a way, that's what happened, but it was far from romantic. It was experimental. He was handsome and I curious about what all the chatter was about. I wanted to understand the songs about love and sex. I wanted to feel the cultural moment.

And so I did.

I was fourteen when I was in the car with Charles. He pulled over so we could kiss on the side of the road, just down from his house. At least that's what I thought was about to happen. Normally, he'd come over to my house and we'd secretly make out on the couch, trying to kiss while keeping an ear out for my parents. My daddy used to pitch a shoe on the floor of the living room, from all the way down the hall. That meant, "It's time for

Charles to go." But on this night, we were all alone in a car. It was approaching my curfew, but we had time for just a little romance.

We climbed in the back seat and began kissing, and pretty soon things got out of hand. I lost my virginity at age fourteen. Right after the act was over, I was filled with shame. *What had I done?* I was in a panic as I watched the dial on my watch meet, then pass my curfew. I'd never missed curfew before.

When Charles dropped me off and I walked up to the house, the lights were off. That was a good sign. I tried to slide into the house, thinking I could tiptoe back to my room and my parents would never know.

Then the lights turned on, revealing that my daddy was standing there with a belt.

"Where have you been?"

Normally I would've thought something up—but what I had prepared flew out of my head. I couldn't even speak, because I was still in shock over what I had just done.

He gave me a whupping, but I didn't cry. This upset my daddy even more, that I wouldn't answer his questions about where I had been. Part of me wanted to get beaten. In my mind at the time, I believed I had made so much of a mistake that I deserved this.

He kept whupping me, until my mama stepped in. "Raymond, that's enough."

He looked at her, then at me. "Get out," he said. I had taken my father to the breaking point and knew I had to obey. I walked out onto the porch, shut the door behind me, and sat down. Though he wanted me to leave, I had nowhere to go in rural Mississippi in the middle of the night. When my mama came out and I saw the kindness in her eyes, I started crying. She started crying too.

"Come on back in," she said.

And I did. The next morning, I stopped wearing those fast-looking clothes. My "liberated" days were over. Even though I was no longer actually innocent, I wanted to look innocent. And I wanted to do enough good things to possibly cancel out the bad I had done. I did errands around the house: I washed dishes, washed the clothes, ironed my father's clothes, and polished his shoes. My parents couldn't come up with a chore I wouldn't do.

I lost something about myself that night: my carefree spirit. Though I loved to make people laugh, I made up my mind that I wasn't going to live in sin. I still saw Charles, but it wasn't the same. I didn't let him come over to the house, and I couldn't go out, since I was grounded. We talked on the phone and saw each other at school. But even that was a bit too much. Every time I looked him in the eyes, he was a reminder of my shame. With thoughts of attending a new integrated school, I was thinking more seriously about my life. I'd never gone to school with white people before, and I needed to figure out exactly how I was going to live my life.

All my good efforts, however, couldn't erase a tiny little reality that had begun that night in the back seat of the car. Three months after I turned fifteen, I suspected I was pregnant. I counted on my fingers, trying desperately to find some error of math that would mean I'd be okay. Being an unwed mama in rural Mississippi in the 1970s was not an option. Not in my town. It would have been such an embarrassment to my family. I was just so young. I would have to go forward at church and confess my sin of being an unwed mother. My high school would kick me out. This wasn't a time when educators wanted to give pregnant teens the best chance at success in life. They believed that exposing others to such sin would be corrupting. Teen mothers were sent back home, usually without explanation. They would have the baby and then often live their quiet lives without a high school degree. Out of sight, out of mind. This would devastate my parents, who so valued education.

I put *A Tale of Two Cities* facedown on my bed, unable to focus on the Charles Dickens book I was reading for school. I fingered the edge of the quilt my mama had made. Panic rose in my chest as I plopped down on my pillow. On the radio, the Isley Brothers sang, "It's your thing, do what you wanna do," but I didn't need them to tell me that. I'd been doing exactly what I wanted to do. That's how I'd gotten into this mess.

I lay there as the evening turned to night, then morning. And the next day, I put on my clothing and went to school like nothing was wrong. I knew I was pregnant, but I couldn't face that quite yet. I definitely couldn't tell Charles. Maybe if I ignored it, everything would be just fine.

One week into my new school year, my mama appeared in the doorway. She looked at me knowingly, biting her lower lip. It was Monday. She was standing by my dresser. "Marie, you're pregnant," she said.

"No I'm not," I said.

"Don't lie to me," she said. "You done messed around and got pregnant."

I nodded, because there was no use in denying it. She and I both burst into tears.

By this time, my daddy had heard our raised voices and had come back to my room.

"What's going on?" he asked, looking at her, then at me.

"She laid up and got pregnant," Mama said. When she told my daddy, I felt sick. I am not sure what I expected his reaction to be. I didn't expect him to start crying too. Then he simply walked away without saying a word. Mama left, so they could discuss my situation.

I could tell they blamed themselves for not being as attentive as perhaps they only then realized they should have been. Though we were a very tight-knit family, we didn't sit down and have big discussions about the complications of life. Most of the "big lessons" I learned were through eavesdropping and—now, I guess I could add—"trial and error." At one point, I tried to talk to my father, but he was so hurt he simply dropped his head. So I went to see if Mama would talk, but she looked away from me.

We'd had a big explosion, followed by silence. That silence was the hardest part. Mama would tell Julius, "Tell your sister to go get that kitchen clean." Or she'd tell Patricia, "Tell your sister to do the laundry."

For two excruciating days, my parents whispered, cried, and spoke in low voices. I just had to get out of the house. I walked outside and took a left turn out of our driveway, hoping the fresh air might miraculously help me feel better. That's when a neighbor, in whom my mama had apparently confided, saw me walking. She pulled her car alongside me and rolled down the window.

"Marie, I heard what happened," she told me. Then her voice dropped. "I can have that fixed for you." Though I so desperately wanted to be a carefree kid, I couldn't agree to an abortion. Not after I'd felt that little baby flutter around inside me.

Then, on Wednesday, the fog lifted. Daddy was going about his work, and Mama was flitting around the house. Normally she enlisted me to help her with housework, so I felt a relief of familiarity when she plopped down a stack of paper in front of me and said, "Fill these out. Address these envelopes."

Eagerly, I sat at the table, looking at what I saw to be envelopes, along with a list of names and addresses. Those were the first words spoken to me in two days. Since she'd asked me to help her with a project, things couldn't be all bad. Though I still didn't know what to do about the baby, at least I could have my mama back.

I labeled the first envelope with the name I recognized as a neighbor, careful to use beautiful, cursive handwriting. I wanted to do right by my mama, to stay on her good side. I had no idea what my life was going to look like going forward, but I knew that this chore indicated Mama had accepted me back as a part of the fold. I wrote, making a tidy stack of envelopes on the table beside me as Mama was preparing food. When I saw her heading down the hall, however, curiosity got the best of me.

Silently and quickly, I opened up one of the envelopes to see what task I was helping Mama accomplish. To my astonishment, I saw the words "You are invited," and then I saw my name on the card. And then the name of Charles Johnson.

A wedding announcement.

My own.

The card shook in my hands, and I hurriedly tried to stuff it back into the envelope before my mama caught me snooping. I laid the envelope on the table. I'd been inviting my friends and neighbors to my own wedding ceremony that I didn't even know was happening.

Though I kind of loved Charles, I wouldn't have selected him as my husband. When was I going to find out about this wedding? Would I have just awakened one day and been driven to the church? Would it even be at the church? Since I didn't really know anything about the wedding that my parents—and apparently Charles's parents—were hoping to pull off, I took a deep breath and slowly reopened the envelope. I slid out the invitation to discover the details of my wedding.

One detail, in particular, mattered more than the others. My eyes ran down the card and read the language under our names. I was going to be married at our house, not at the church. Then I found the detail I really needed.

According to the invitation, I was getting married on Saturday. In three days.

I had to run away.

When my mama left the house, I dialed the number of my mother's sister. She lived in Houston, which seemed just far enough away to do the trick.

Please answer the phone, please answer the phone.

When I heard her voice, I let out a huge sigh of relief. "Aunt Jessie Mae, this is Marie," I began. "You have to help me."

"Slow down," she said. I wasn't sure how she'd respond, since she was, after all, my mama's sister. After I explained the situation,

I stopped talking and waited to hear what she'd say. Turns out, very few people in America were too thrilled about the idea of a forced marriage. Only after she agreed to help did I realize I had been holding my breath.

"I'll buy a bus ticket for you," she said, before hanging up. Olive Branch didn't have a bus stop, but I could figure out a way to catch it in Memphis. Then I called my older sister Celestine, who lived in Memphis and could probably help get me where I needed to go. I loved spending some nights and weekends with her, to help her take care of her babies. Celestine was one of the only people to whom I would tell my secrets.

"I know you don't want to hear this, but getting married is probably the best thing," she said after I told her my news. "You don't want people calling your baby names." I hadn't thought of that, but unflattering nicknames aimed at a baby by uncharitable people were the least of my worries.

"I'm scared," I said. I'd told Celestine everything about my life since I was young. Even though we were fourteen years apart, I felt like I could tell her anything. And so I did. "I'm going to run away to Houston."

"Marie, you can't leave," she said, her voice certain. "That would hurt everybody."

"I have to," I told her. Whether or not she was going to help, I knew I was leaving. When I told her goodbye, I wondered when I would see her again.

After I hung up the phone, I ran to my room and shut the door. I rummaged through my drawers and swept up clothes. Would I miss Mississippi? My parents? Of course I would, but I had no choice. I swallowed back tears as I stuffed clothes and underwear into a suitcase. But in a few minutes, Julius showed up at my door.

"Going somewhere?" he asked, leaning on the door. I didn't realize he was standing there, watching me. I jumped.

"You can't stop me," I said.

"That's exactly what I'm going to do," he said. "Mama's orders."

"You better get out of my way, before I knock you out of the way."

"I don't fight pregnant girls," he said, "but you're not going anywhere."

Celestine had called my mama just as soon as we'd hung up the phone. And—like dominoes falling—Mama had alerted Julius. Julius had showed up to stop me. I plopped on the bed, officially out of options and utterly depressed that Celestine had betrayed me.

Over the next few days, we bought cheap rings and made decorations. Something about all the activity made me wonder if this might be the right decision after all. By the time Saturday arrived, I had accepted my plight. I awakened when Mama knocked on the door and handed me a dress that my first cousin had worn for prom. It was white. Pretty, actually. It reminded me of getting baptized, but this was going to be a very different type of baptism. One of pain. I blinked back tears as I put it on and looked in the mirror. I looked good, like a typical bride except that I appeared even younger in the wedding dress. I'd never guessed that I'd be wearing one at fifteen years of age, especially since no one had ever asked me to get married. No one had asked me if I even *wanted* to get married.

"You ready?" my mama asked, smiling at me. And, in spite of all my plans for my future going up in smoke, I nodded.

We had made a chicken-wire arch that we filled with tissue paper flowers we'd made over the previous few days. We stood the arch on the front lawn. There, a minister friend of the Johnsons, the Reverend Clark, stood before all our loved ones. They were smiling, holding handkerchiefs, and looking at me through tear-filled eyes. My daddy took me by the arm, walked me to the front, and gave me away to this teenage boy best known for his trumpet playing and dance moves.

What have I done?

"We are gathered here today to join this woman and this man in holy matrimony," said the pastor. No one laughed at his use of the terms "woman" and "man."

"If anyone can show just cause why this couple cannot lawfully be joined together in matrimony, let them speak now or forever hold their peace."

I took a deep breath and turned my head to look at all who had assembled on our lawn. No one objected to our marriage when the pastor gave them the opportunity to throw their hands in the air and say "Stop!"

Not even me.

∞∞∞∞∞∞∞∞

My high school experience was quite different from my friends'.

The school administrators told me that I would no longer be allowed to attend school, and so I spent my days at home. Rather, at Charles's home.

After the wedding, I had to leave my brother, sisters, and parents, and move into the home of Charles. Though his parents were kind to me, I was desperately lonely. I helped clean around the house and even began cooking for them. They weren't used to good food like my mama had taught me to create, so they appreciated having this young girl living with them who could perform domestic tasks.

As a way for me to keep up with what was going on in the tenth grade, my friend Alma brought me her books and her old tests. I would teach myself the material and then take her quizzes myself. My pregnancy was relatively uneventful. On December 20, 1970, I had a baby girl. I named her Tretessa, after a French novel I'd been reading. After I delivered her, my husband and I moved into a house adjacent to my parents' property so they could help me with the baby. But I couldn't just sit back and accept the fact that the school board had banished me from school. I decided to approach them to plead my case.

"How am I supposed to have a future without a high school diploma?" I asked the school administrators.

I could tell by the looks in their eyes what was going through their minds: *You should've thought about that earlier, young lady.* Yet I was persistent.

"How old is your baby?" one of the board members asked. But I could tell by the edge in his voice he wasn't asking out of curiosity. "You need to be home with that child."

Since he was trying to get me to drop out, I didn't even honor him with an answer.

"All right," one of the administrators said. "You can go back to the tenth grade, but you can't progress to the eleventh."

But I was prepared for that fight. "I have enough credits to skip tenth and still be able to graduate."

"You aren't ready to be a junior," he said.

"I know all the curriculum for the tenth grade," I protested.

My mama vouched for me. "I've been seeing her hitting the books."

Finally, with much reluctance, they agreed to let me take one test that covered all the material for the entire year. If I passed it, they'd let me move on to eleventh grade. It felt less like an act of generosity and more of a trick to get me to stop asking them. They didn't think it could be done, especially since they scheduled the test for three days later.

The administration asked teachers from another school to put together a test on their respective subjects. Each subject had over a hundred questions. On the day of the test, I knew I could handle it. It took me four hours, and I made a 98 percent on it.

I was officially a high school junior.

Going back to high school and leaving my daughter was tough, but I had looked forward to returning for months. When I got there, everything had changed. My friends were obsessed with boys and fashion, while I was thinking about bottles and diapers. My friends didn't tell me everything they used to tell me. And when they did, their gossip just felt childish. Of course, they hadn't changed. They were exactly the way high school kids should've been. I was the one who had changed. There was no going back to the way life was before I was married.

Charles didn't have the same feeling. He continued to go out at night, basically living the life of a single high school kid. I kept my head down and studied, making good grades and trying to be a good wife. In a way, my whole marriage was orchestrated to save me from the embarrassment of "going forward" at church, a "walk of shame" that ideally allows sinful Christians the opportunity to confess their sins. I, of course, would've had to confess that I'd had sex outside marriage, an embarrassment for me and my family (though in retrospect, it wouldn't have been as embarrassing as all the drama that later came from my marriage). Though I knew that confession was good for the soul, I didn't want to do that.

Since I'd turned my back on the church earlier in life, I didn't take my children to church like my parents had taken us kids. However, they knew about Jesus, because I told them all about Him. I wanted a good, solid family, and even though I had a rocky marital beginning, I set out to create one.

When I was midway into my junior year, I realized I was pregnant again. Tretessa was only eleven months old. My baby's new due date would be in August. This time, I vowed, I wasn't going to tell anybody. I knew the principal would kick me out of school if he knew I was having another baby. (This is even though I was married.) And so I wore baggy clothes, studied hard, and kept the news within the family.

One month before my baby was due, my mama knocked on the door with a concerned look on her face.

"I just got off the phone with Mrs. Ray," she said. "You should sit down." I could tell by her stricken face that this was serious.

"What'd she want?" I asked. Mrs. Ray was the mama of a girl at our school named Joyce. I wasn't close friends with her daughter.

"She told me Charles comes by the house all the time," she said, enunciating each word. "And that Joyce is his girlfriend. She wanted to tell me in the hopes that he'll stop coming around."

My heart started thudding in my chest, my head started thumping, my throat went bone dry. I just couldn't believe it. After I left my mother, I went into the bathroom and found some of her pills. I didn't want to kill myself, but I wanted the pain in my heart to go away. I took one, then another. I don't recall how many I ultimately swallowed, but it was enough to make the pain stop temporarily. The next thing I remember, I was in the back of an ambulance with medics hovering over me.

"Wake up," they said. "Open your eyes."

The betrayal was too much to bear. When I asked Charles about the affair, he simply denied it. We had another daughter, who arrived on August 15. I named her Catina, but I kept the news of her arrival—her existence—within the family. Even my closest friends didn't know I had two children.

By this time, I had enough credits to get out of school at noon. That meant that every afternoon, I was able to get on a bus and go to vocational-technical school. At the time, Sawyers Secretarial School was teaching a typing-skills class. I hoped that learning a skill would help me make a living, but I didn't tell my husband. I knew Charles would object to these lessons, since he seemed generally opposed to anything that reeked of self-improvement and advancement.

By the time graduation rolled around, I had accomplished a great deal. As they were announcing the scholarships, they called my name. To my surprise, I had been given a band scholarship, because of my oboe skills. The idea of going away for a four-year college degree, of course, was so enticing. But even as I let my mind wander, I caught Charles's eye. "Don't even think about it," he mouthed.

Then they went on to announce that Sawyers Secretarial School was giving me an award. Not only had I never missed a class, I could type ninety-one words per minute when I graduated. I walked up to the podium to get the award. My husband, sitting in the front row, shook his head in disbelief. Though the audience applauded for me, all I could see was the look of disapproval on his face.

After graduation, my friends gathered around to congratulate me. When they saw me standing with my family, they were shocked to see that I had two children.

After I graduated, I interviewed for a secretarial position at Keene Lighting, the same place my daddy had worked for years. When the boss there realized how quickly I could type, I was hired on the spot. The fact that I had an in-house job at this company was a source of great pride for my daddy and for me. Plus, I was the first black woman in Olive Branch to hold an office job.

I'd done it. I'd done everything that was in my control to create a good life for my husband and family.

But soon I'd learn that life sometimes spirals out of control anyway.

Chapter 4

I was exhausted.

After Tretessa and Catina were born, I had another baby named Charles and another one named Bryant, who arrived thirteen months later. We lived in a house that didn't have any running water—yes, Mississippi still had houses like that back then. One day, I lay down on the bed to rest my eyes with my baby. After I dozed off, I awakened with a start. My head was hot. I opened my eyes and sat straight up. In the mirror, I saw my hair was on fire. Out of the corner of my eye, I saw little Charles, only about fifteen months old at the time. He had turned tail and was running away.

Always curious about fire, Charles had seen me light the space heater. When I fell asleep, he'd gone over to light the fire by himself. I don't know how this happened, but presumably he lit a long piece of wood and it began to burn his hand. At that point, he probably tossed it to me, and it had lit my hair. Since we had no running water, it's a good thing that I was in the bed. I used the quilt to pat the fire out.

After it was all over, my hair still hot and completely singed, I checked on Charles to make sure he wasn't also aflame. His fingers were blackened, but he was otherwise fine. I held him in my arms.

"Maybe one day," I said, "you'll be a firefighter."

I'd long ago had to leave my job at Keene Lighting, because it had shut down. I'd had a series of other jobs, but after my most recent company shutdown, I was jobless once more. To make matters worse, I discovered I was pregnant again. My fifth. I couldn't believe it. Ever since I learned of Charles's relationship with my high school classmate Joyce, he had continued to be unfaithful. Humiliated by his infidelity, I didn't even tell him I was expecting.

I had to leave.

In 1979, I found a small apartment in Memphis and welcomed my final baby into this world. I named him Cory, which somehow changed into Coconut and then was shortened to Coco. As soon as he was close to being weaned off the bottle, I went down to the local welfare office and filled out the forms so I could receive government assistance. I didn't trust anyone to keep my children, so they were always with me. As I held their chubby little hands in the food stamp line, I noticed some of the people ahead of me were there with their parents and grandparents. Multigenerational dependence on welfare was not what I wanted for my kids. What was I passing down to my children?

"I hate this. I need to find a job," I said one day to one of the women in social services. "Do you know of any openings?"

She looked at me sideways. "You do realize that public assistance was created to help people like you, right?"

"I don't want my children to see that this is an option," I said. "Standing in line and getting free money?"

"Welfare is for people going through a transition," she said. But I didn't feel right about taking this public assistance. My family didn't do welfare. Every time I saw her, I mentioned I needed to get a job and a paycheck, to be a good role model for my children. And, without fail, she assured me that me taking public assistance was a good temporary solution for my circumstances.

"But I want to change my circumstance," I told her. "I want my children to expect more out of life than this."

She paused and looked down at her fingernails. Finally, she smiled. "All right," she said. "What can you do?"

"Type and office work."

"I did hear about a job at the Urban League," she said, writing the address down on a piece of paper. I tried not to grab it from her hands. The Urban League helped expand the economic opportunities for poor people, and having a nine-to-five would definitely expand my economic opportunities. I interviewed for the job and landed it. Finally, self-sufficient. Though I desired the peace and stability of a traditional family, staying with Charles for so many years hadn't yet magically transformed our marriage into something stable. I left him many times, only to return again. I guess this is the plight of many women, being unable to leave a bad circumstance because of fear, uncertainty, and few options. This time, I told myself, I was really done.

I needed to dress professionally but I had only four pieces of clothing, which I wore in different configurations until I went to Goodwill and probably bought a few more outfits with large shoulder pads—it was 1980, after all. I settled in to my new job at the Urban League as a receptionist and a secretary. I'd been there only a few months when one of my coworkers ran into the office with news about another coworker.

"Greg was killed in a tragic accident," she said, tears running down her face.

People in the office began crying hysterically, but I dealt with my own grief through writing. I stayed at my desk and wrote a beautiful poem commemorating his life, examining what it felt like to be missing him. I knew that he was an only child, and I hated to think about the grief of his mother.

"May I?" asked one of my coworkers, when she saw what I had written. I handed her my sheet of paper and watched her face soften as she read the words.

"This is just beautiful," she said, sniffing. "Do you care if I read this at the board meeting tonight?" Of course I allowed it. One of the people on the board was the vice president of FedEx, who was so touched by the poem that he sent for me.

"Are you the one who wrote this?" he asked, clutching the piece of paper.

I nodded.

"Do you mind if I send it to Greg's mother?"

"I'd be honored." I was even more honored when they asked if they could use it as part of the program at his funeral. A few days later, the vice president found me again.

"Alice, would you like to work at FedEx? I believe I could use someone like you."

I didn't answer at first. In my head ran a proverb from the

Bible. It read, "A man's gift makes room for him, and brings him before great men."[1] And there I was, getting an audience before this executive who controlled access to some of the most coveted jobs in Memphis. The gift God gave me—writing—was enabling me to go further than I had ever hoped.

"Would I?" I asked, not even trying to hide my enthusiasm. "Of course."

And so I received an office job and was put into the clerical pool. There I met Harvey Mae Garner, who is still my lifetime friend. We laughed so much and had more fun than anyone deserved to have at work. She had lost both her parents, and so my family folded her and her two kids into our family—this brought joy back into the holidays for her. My daddy would pull her kids around in a wagon on the Fourth of July as if they were his own grandchildren. After six months, I got promoted to the revenue recovery department.

While I was there, I showed a pattern of discrimination against FedEx employees who were women and people of color. I wrote a grievance about the issue, after having collected evidence. And my boss took note. He stood in front of my desk and told me that I'd never get promoted in that department due to my actions. On the day that my grievance was to be heard, I expected to see a human resource representative, as FedEx's internal policies required. Lo and behold, the personnel rep who walked in was none other than Jim Perkins, the vice president and the global head of personnel.

---

[1] Proverbs 18:16 (New King James Version).

To everyone's surprise, he came up to me and said, "Hi, Alice, how are you doing?"

The room went dead silent.

"I'm doing well, Jim," I replied, lifting up my chin ever so slightly.

He smiled and told everyone in the room to take a seat. He told us he'd looked at the evidence and thought I'd brought up some good points. No one moved, but my heart soared. Then he turned to me and asked for my advice on how to make things right.

"This is not just about me," I said. I was more interested in helping others who might have been affected. After the meeting, he promoted people from lower-level positions to entry-level exempt positions. This applied all over Memphis and the nation. When the news came out, people erupted in celebration. The employees put their phones on mute, everybody shouted. The occupational opportunities for my dear friends, such as Willie Patterson, were blasted wide open. (By the way, he's now a senior manager at FedEx.)

That same week, I received notification that I had been selected as one of four managers in a new department in computer operations. After three years in that department, I was promoted again to a higher level of management in customer support. I started the first quality action teams at FedEx, spoke at their conferences, and facilitated a class called "Is Management for Me?" I wanted to empower people, especially women, to achieve greater things than they thought they could. I even taught the other employees, like my friend and coordinator Gloria Brooks, how to prepare for a management position on my own time. My bosses took notice.

At Christmas, I got an award for being one of the best managers, because I showed concern for other people's careers, helped with their résumés, and provided counsel on getting ahead.

In the meantime, I'd gotten back with Charles. Why? It's hard for me to describe the complicated relationship I had with my husband. I know for sure that we married too young, and that neither he nor I was ready for such a commitment. I don't blame him for that. Because of our immaturity—among other factors—our marriage was not stable. It ebbed and flowed. Though I worked up the courage to leave him on occasion, I'd invariably come back. I missed him. I loved him. And above all, I wanted my children to have a father and to all share the same last name. As I reflect back on my reasoning now with more spiritual maturity, I can see that I was naive to hope he'd change or that we could magically transform into a happy couple. But I didn't know that then. Our marriage was on-again, off-again, as I tried in spite of everything to make us into one big, happy family.

But happiness was hard to come by—a lesson I would learn repeatedly.

During the last snow of the year on March 7, 1984, I dropped my friend Delores Crutcher off at her home. I didn't put my seat belt back on, because my house was the next street over.

Out of nowhere, a car sideswiped my older-model green-and-white car, and I hit a stone telephone pole. At the point of impact, my face slammed into the steering wheel and my body was thrust into the floorboard. I was in a fog of pain. When I came to my senses, my head hung on the floor on the passenger's side. Then the gigantic pole fell on my car, crushing what was left of it to the ground. My mandible (the bone that holds the bottom teeth) was broken and lodged at the back of my mouth. My teeth felt loose. I tried to get out of the car, but I was trapped in a cage of metal.

My pain was so severe that I couldn't quite hear anything. Then I heard sirens and the sound of the medics discussing what they saw.

"Whoever was in this car probably didn't survive," a person said while he inserted a mechanical device to detect my heartbeat.

I heard him scream an expletive. "Somebody's alive in here!"

I was going in and out of consciousness. In the meantime, some neighbors had recognized my ugly car and had gone to my house. When my husband came to the door—this was during an "on-again" phase—they told him they'd seen my car in a terrible accident.

"Alice had the car," he said, taking off to go to the accident.

Things at the scene were pretty harrowing.

"Whoever's in there, you're going to be okay," I heard a voice urgently say. I heard them barking orders to get the Jaws of Life to pull me out of my car. "Stay with us."

I'm not sure how long I was trapped, because I went into shock. When I finally was freed from the wreckage, my mother and family had arrived at the scene of the accident. When my mother saw my face, she screamed. That's when I knew things were bad. I opened my mouth to speak to her, but my teeth were loose. I spit out some of my teeth to avoid swallowing them.

The medics put me into an ambulance and rushed me to the hospital, where I underwent immediate surgery. For months, I had to wear a cast over my remaining bottom teeth, which were secured by screws fastened on the outside of the bottom of my jaw. I was given a bottom partial denture. I was told my lack of a seat belt actually saved my life, because it allowed me to slide below the main point of impact. Though I was so thankful that I'd survived, I was devastated that I'd lost so many of my teeth.

Dental hygiene was always important to my parents, because they knew that having bad teeth reflected poorly on your image. After I'd angered the dentist who had watered down my dose of novocaine, it put me in a bind since he said never to bring me back. And so I always took good care of my teeth, as a way to counteract his hatred. *I'll show him*, I thought, as I brushed.

I never expected this.

Thankfully at FedEx I had a pretty good salary. I decided to get the dental work I needed. Dental implants were the best option, an expensive procedure that surgically connected the dental prostheses to the bone of my jaw as an anchor so that I could have permanent teeth once again. Because of the cost and the amount of healing that needed to take place, it took years to get them all done. But, finally, I had my smile fully restored and my mouth looked perfect.

Well, as perfect as I wanted it to look.

Once I had a cavity in the very back of my mouth, and I told the dentist to put a gold crown on it. Back then, everyone was wearing gold teeth, but that look didn't appeal to me. But I thought it would be funny to have one in the back of my mouth as a joke. When I'd hang out with my close friends, we'd get to talking and cracking each other up. That's when I'd throw back my head and go into full-throated laughter. Only then might they see the tooth and laugh even louder.

"Alice, I can't believe you have a gold tooth," they'd exclaim, which would make me laugh even more. It was something about myself that I loved, because it was so surprising and uncharacteristic for me to have it. That gold tooth in the back of my mouth was just a little secret joke that I'd share with people I was close to.

◇◇◇◇◇◇◇◇◇◇

By this time, Charles had already had two children by two other women. In spite of my best efforts (and wishful thinking), things had not improved. One night, he didn't come home, but I stayed up waiting. The sun had already come up by the time he arrived home, so I met him in the driveway and climbed in the passenger side of his car. "I know you have other children," I said. "I can't change that. But I can't live like this. I want a family, a father here with us, and I want to be happy. If you want to be with this woman, go be with her. If you want to stay here with us, we want you back. But the choice is yours."

He paused to think about it. There was something about that pause that settled something in my soul. The love that I'd felt disappeared. I didn't want to be married to a man who had to think about whether or not he wanted to be with me, and me alone. In spite of all the years of lies, he had one moment when he told me the truth.

"I don't know what I want," he said. "I care for both of you."

I knew then he was not going to change. "You just made your choice. Come back tomorrow. I'll pack up your things."

After fourteen years of legal matrimony (though not "holy matrimony"), I filed for divorce. It would take over five years to go through, but I no longer felt like Charles Johnson's wife. It was hard, but necessary. I kept the name Johnson because I wanted to make sure I had the same last name as my children.

In 1987, after being legally separated from Charles for three years, I met a new friend, a man named Ted, through a coworker. He was married and had one child, but he intrigued me from the moment I asked him what he did for a living. He told me he was a professional gambler.

"What's your game?" I asked.

"I don't have a game, I have a race." During this time, greyhound racing was a very popular pastime, and the dog tracks would attract thousands of gamblers on the weekends. Every year, over $200 million was wagered on the dogs, and Ted was a part of it. "I handicap dogs."

I didn't understand it, but he introduced me to the world of greyhound racetracks. One popular spot was just across the Mississippi River in West Memphis, a particularly vibrant scene. I loved the funny names of the dogs, the men writing on pads, crunching numbers, handing over fistfuls of cash. Though Ted had a serious strategy, I bet on dogs with names I liked—at least at first. He taught me the basics, and I found it was more fun to cheer for "my" dog as he raced after the "rabbit." This actually was just a mechanical lure: a stick with a gray foam bone on the end that the dogs never caught by design. We celebrated when Ted's selections would win, place, or show.

Though I'd been wounded so badly by infidelity, I had an affair with Ted. I made excuses that seared my conscience to his marital status. It even gave me a little insulation. I knew he wouldn't show up wanting more from me than I wanted to give. He wouldn't show up one day on the doorstep with a suitcase and a toothbrush. And so I let him into my life and into my bed.

It was a terrible decision that would change the course of my life forever.

I thought I could sin a little here and a little there. I thought I could keep my sin in a little box in my life and take it out when I wanted it. I thought it would stay put, stay contained. But instead, my bad decisions began to compound and sin began to expand until there was so much of it that the box overflowed.

I'd read James 1:15 before, but I hadn't heeded the scripture's warning. "Then when lust hath conceived, it bringeth forth sin: and sin, when it is finished, bringeth forth death." I didn't die, but in the Old Testament the Hebrew word for death means "separation." When I was sentenced to life in prison, that separation became real to me. You never really believe that a little sin can cause such chaos, but that's the way it works. Once I made the bad decision to have an affair, the bad decisions multiplied.

Ted introduced me to gambling, and I got absolutely hooked on the thrill of the risk and the surge of the win. For the first time in many years, I experienced carefree fun. It was the first time I'd felt like a true free spirit since I'd married Charles. For years I'd been working hard and raising kids. So much of my life had been devoted to taking care of my family that there was little I did for myself, let alone times that I allowed myself to have fun like this. It was almost like I was trying to replicate the joy I'd lost from my childhood being cut short.

Of course, that was all an illusion, because the fun came at a high price. Though sometimes we'd hit it big, the losses also began to pile up. It didn't make sense to actually put real money on these dogs, but a combination of greed, risk, and fun caused me to get deeper and deeper into that lifestyle. I began to get behind on some of my bills.

After five years of separation, my divorce became final. To my surprise, it had a bigger emotional impact on me than I expected. I knew it was over between us, but I grieved the loss of my childhood sweetheart.

Thankfully, my job at FedEx was going better than ever. Through my influence as a manager, I had been able to get Dolores and Julius jobs. My family is a huge success story—from sharecroppers to educated people with good-paying jobs—and I could tell they were proud of how far I'd gone. That is, until my worlds collided in the worst possible way.

It all started because I was supposed to go on a work trip that would cost the company quite a bit of money. On trips like these, the company would advance me the cash, so my travel expenses would not be out of pocket. I'd already gotten my cash advance for the trip when I learned it had been canceled. The trip was off, but I still had the money. And as bad luck would have it, Ted and I had just hit a losing streak at the racetracks.

"I have thirty days to file my expense report," I mentioned to

Ted. The money wasn't mine, but with my increasing amount of gambling debt, it felt good to hold it in my hands.

"Can I borrow it?" he asked. "I just need it for a few days, and I'll have it back to you well before it's time to file the expense report." He told me he'd have it back to me in no time.

I knew it would be extremely unethical, since it wasn't my money to give. However, he assured me it would be covered and I could use some of it to help me get out of my debt. "Okay, but I need it as soon as possible," I told him.

And just like that, I added another item to my list of sins.

I saw him a few days later, and he noticed the worried expression on my face.

"You don't expect it back yet," he teased. "It's coming." I still had plenty of time before I had to file the report, so I put it out of my mind. But when another week passed, and another, I felt like my stomach was going to fold in on itself.

"I need the money," I said to him over the phone, this time more urgently.

Two days before the deadline, I began to utterly panic. Had I simply gone to my family, they would've fussed about it but helped me out. But my family didn't know about my gambling addiction, and I was ashamed. I didn't want them to know how dire my situation actually was. And so, I plastered a smile on my face and tried to keep up the facade of success. There was no way I'd tell my respectable, upright family that I'd made a $5,000 mistake.

"I'll drop it off in the morning," Ted promised, and I let myself feel a little relief. But when the morning came, he didn't. I knew I'd been compromised. I had a stack of bills on the counter, and I'd been dodging bill collectors for weeks. When they called, I changed my voice to make myself sound like a man or a child. Whatever it took; I didn't want the bill collector to know he was talking to me. I didn't want to hear about the debt I owed. Every time I opened the mailbox, bills and late notices marked in red ink fell out. Christmas was fast approaching.

I officially missed the deadline on the travel reimbursement, which meant I'd embezzled money from my employer. When FedEx realized I hadn't even gone on the trip, they opened an investigation. Before I knew it, they brought me into personnel, who grilled me on what I'd done. It was so embarrassing to come face-to-face with my greed and deception. When the meeting ended, they fired me. Bad news spread quickly, and soon all my coworkers saw me gathering my personal belongings. I did the walk of shame out to the parking lot.

Ten years of work, gone in an instant. My heart was racing. And, like dogs at the track, I still didn't realize I'd never catch the rabbit in this gambling game. Since I needed the money even more, I looked to the races, hoping for a big win.

Sin always promises what it can't deliver. When I first had my affair with Ted, sin offered me love but gave me heartbreak. When I first gambled on the dog races, sin offered me riches but gave me poverty. When I first decided to lend Ted the money, sin offered a feeling of importance but gave me unemployment. Sin's lies always sounded good to my carnal ears, but they resulted in the death of something in my life.

But I hadn't learned yet not to rely on sin's lies.

Within weeks, I'd filed for bankruptcy, and my house was about to be foreclosed on. My car had been repossessed. After a couple of months of unemployment, I finally got a job as a factory worker at Kellogg's. My parents bought me an old Ford Taurus for $1,000, which allowed me to reliably go to and from work. However, I still didn't make enough to make ends meet, and I couldn't catch up on what I owed. I also had a daughter in college and the second one getting ready to go into college. After Charles and I separated, I cared for all five children, and Charles didn't pay a dime of child support. As the days rolled by, and very little money rolled in, the prospect of not having a home was looming. I tried to call Charles and ask for help, but I looked for him and couldn't find him.

One day, after going to the tracks, my cousin pulled me aside. They were there visiting from Houston.

"How are you doing?" she asked. She had concern in her eyes. I told her how I was about to lose the house. Then, as if she was offering a financial solution, she mentioned her husband was looking for someone who could help move drugs.

"Know of anyone who can help?"

"Drugs?" I repeated in disbelief. "Of course not. I don't know anyone who sells drugs."

"Well, if you *do* know of anybody, would you just let me know?" The way she stressed it lodged into my mind. "If you *do* know of anyone, give me a call."

The next time I saw Ted, I casually mentioned the strange interaction. He had been trying to help me with my bills, but since his income relied on gambling, he wasn't able to help much. "You're not going to believe what my cousin said to me."

"About what?"

"Drugs," I said, laughing. "Can you believe it?"

His eyes widened. "What did she say exactly?"

"She asked me if I knew anyone who sold them."

"What did you say?" he asked.

"What do you think I said?" I laughed. "I don't know anyone who sells drugs."

"I do," he said.

"Who do you know?"

"You're looking at him."

My heart thudded in my chest. I never, ever knew Ted did anything other than gamble.

"Give me her number," he said. "I can make it happen."

I introduced Ted and my cousin, and they asked me to help in a very discreet, simple way. They asked me to pass on information.

"All you have to do is let someone call you, then you call another person and relay the number the first person gives you," Ted said. "Can you do that?"

My involvement was a form of protection. Since I wasn't selling drugs on the streets, no one knew me. The dealers knew only of a voice on the other end of the phone line. I'd give them a number to call, and then someone else would call them. It was a labyrinth designed to confuse any authorities.

I thought about it, but not for long. It was the perfect gig. The drug buyers out on the street and the drug dealers on the phone would never see my face. I wasn't the one out there getting people addicted. I would simply relay information from one person to another. And so, prompted by financial desperation and greed, I did.

Sin was offering me a way out, and I decided to take it. Little did I know that I'd end up paying for this mistake with my very life.

"Here's your take," Ted said a couple of days later, handing me a huge stack of cash.

I took the money and flipped through it. "A thousand dollars? Really?"

"Really," he said, smiling. Though this amount of money might not seem like a big deal to people now, it allowed me to eat and keep my lights on. I gave him a big hug, believing—incorrectly— that I'd found a way out.

Having done it once, I did it again. And again. With the illegal money coming in, at least I grew more responsible with my finances and slowed down on my gambling. I was able to take the money I got illegally and pay down my debts and bills. I would also squirrel money away in an effort to one day buy a house. Then I received some unexpected retirement money from FedEx. They had to pay out on my retirement, something I had not even anticipated as a possibility.

This "clean" money allowed me, in 1992, to fulfill a lifelong dream. Since my mother had been so entrepreneurial, I'd always dreamed of one day following in her footsteps. I took $1,000 of the retirement money and bought into a cleaning company called

ServiceMaster. I needed a legitimate business, and this franchise seemed like a low-entry way to become a business owner. Plus, I liked how the company seemed to honor God in its business practices. Yes, I know it sounds hypocritical, that I'd seek out a God-honoring company on one hand while I was a drug information mule on the other. But, like many people, I compartmentalized my life, building little walls between my sin and virtue and trying to keep them separate.

I was in terrible sin, but I felt a strong urge to go back to church. I'd been separated from church for a long time. I hadn't even raised my children "in the church," at least not in the way that we Boggan kids were raised. I definitely taught my children about Jesus, and they grew to know and love Him through the Bible stories I loved to tell them. But I did realize I lost something important when I left the protection and the authority of the church. I tried out one church, then another. When my parents' church had special days, I'd go. But even though I started going back, regrettably I didn't let it affect my behavior.

With a little help from Ted, I bought a very modest house for $90,000. Now that I had a place to lay my head, I was able to settle in with the kids and try to establish a new normal. I decided to dial back the illegal money I was making and to focus on making money through my new franchise.

Regrettably, however, a new form of gambling came to our area. In the early 1990s, casinos started springing up in Mississippi, and gamblers flocked from the dog tracks to the slot machines to try their luck. Many southerners had not been to actual casinos and got in over their heads—including me. I had thought that I'd been able to tamp down on my gambling addiction, but it was there, latent, waiting for the right moment to rear its ugly head. Even though things had begun to stabilize, and I was now able to pay my bills, I decided to risk it all by going into those flashy casinos and trying my hand at games of chance.

I learned how to play blackjack and poker. And—wow!—I won big. There's nothing quite like the adrenaline rush of winning an unexpectedly large sum of cash simply for playing cards. But it only *seemed* as if I won big. Of course, I didn't take that money and go home. Instead, I used the money to bet again. The next time, I lost. Feeling desperate to get that rush again, I kept putting more money down, and down again, but the spiral continued. My soul felt empty when I walked out of the casino, having lost everything I'd won—and much, much more.

In spite of my gambling, my ServiceMaster job began to grow and thrive. I landed a huge contract even though I didn't follow the conventional wisdom about bidding low to get the job.

There was hope.

◇◇◇◇◇◇◇◇◇

It was in the middle of this confusing time of professional success and bad judgment in my personal life that true tragedy entered my life in the most painful way possible: through one of my children.

There was always something special about my youngest child, Coco. I knew he would definitely be my last child, since I'd gotten a divorce, and I doted on him so much that I felt guilty. It's not that I loved him more than the others, but his soft and affectionate spirit always resonated with me. Though I'd never let the other kids sleep with me, I gave in by the time Coco arrived. Plus, I loved how he and Bryant were as thick as thieves. They were inseparable for as long as I could remember. If you asked either of them, "Who's your best friend?" they would both quickly answer, "My brother."

In October, on my brother's birthday, I was at a cellular service company, trying to work out a problem with my phone. That's when I received a call. Bryant and Coco had been involved in a scooter accident and I needed to get to the hospital immediately.

I went to the hospital as quickly as I could. When I got there, the nurses and doctors had grim looks on their faces. I'd been under the impression that Coco had broken his leg, maybe. Perhaps some ribs. But when I saw their faces, I realized that I'd been terribly wrong.

"Miss Johnson," the doctor said, "we're sorry to have to inform you that . . ."

Honestly, I didn't hear the words. I can't tell you exactly what was said, because my brain didn't absorb it. He told me that my beloved son was already brain dead. Since Charles was nowhere to be found, I had to make the decision about whether to take my son off life support.

My son.

I went into the chapel and began to pray. A sunbeam came down and enveloped me. I felt a release from the Lord, that I needed to go ahead and make the decision to send Coco to God. "Just promise me, Lord, to take care of him until I can get there," I begged.

I gave the instructions to turn off the artificial life assistance, and then I promptly fainted. My sister Coria caught me, and the hospital gave me medication to deal with the trauma of this news. They offered to keep me overnight, but my family agreed to watch after me.

After the medicine calmed my nerves, I went to Bryant. He was bereft, grieving, and in shock. I comforted him as much as I could, but I knew the emotional trauma of seeing his brother die like that would probably never truly leave until heaven. Plus, I had very little capability to comfort him while I was overcome with my own grief. Charles did arrive, but it was too late. Our son had already died.

While I was at the hospital, the phone at my house rang off the hook. Neighbors called, friends called, and family members called, including Coco's cousin, who was married to a man who lived in Colombia. Of course, I wasn't home to receive the many calls. And if I had been there, the last thing I would've done is field phone calls. Thankfully, I had family at the house who faithfully relayed all the information we had. News of Coco's death spread quickly, and the reality began to set in.

I'd lost him.

"I just regret that Coco never got baptized," I lamented.

"What are you talking about?" Bryant asked. "He *was* baptized."

"Well, why didn't I know about it?"

"I barely did," he said. Apparently, in 1991, Coco and Bryant had been attending a summer Bible education series, and several people were getting baptized. Coco made the spur-of-the-moment decision to be baptized too. He counseled with the pastor, who allowed him to be baptized. There was no mourning bench, no emotional public proclamations. He was just a good kid who wanted to quietly do what was right. And I was proud of him for taking this path, even while his parents' marriage was deteriorating, even when our family was in disarray. This news was a huge comfort in all of my misery.

My daughters and my sisters, thankfully, stepped in where I could not, and took care of the funeral arrangements. The cost of the funeral, the casket, and other burial expenses added to my ever-growing list of debts. But I didn't care about that. I couldn't care. What is financial debt when compared with the loss of life?

For about six months, I very seldom came out of my room. Everyone in my house was silent. Even my own children tiptoed around. In my grief, I didn't let anyone pack up Coco's clothes, even though his brothers were still in that room. I regret that now, but these were the decisions a woman who was out of her mind with grief made. In retrospect, I wish I had gotten the kids grief counseling, especially Bryant. I wish I'd been more emotionally available to my children when they needed me most.

It took me almost ten years to even look at a picture of Coco, and almost as long for me to be able to speak his name.

I plunged into deep despair.

Then, unimaginably, things got even worse.

Chapter 5

"This is how he can reach me," a woman's voice said on the other end of the line. It was September, and I was doing what I did: passing info along for drug dealers. The woman said she was in Tunica, Mississippi. When the call ended, I called Ted.

"This is the number," I said. Then I turned over and went back to sleep. Unbeknownst to me, I'd sent Ted into a trap. When he made it to the hotel, he was arrested, though the woman was nowhere to be seen.

Hours later, it was still dark when the police came and knocked on my door. "We want you to come down to the police station," they said, indicating it was not optional. "Ted has been arrested."

My eyes were as wide as saucers, but I complied. They brought me in, took me into a room, and threatened me. "If you don't cooperate," one officer said, "we're going to arrest your daughter."

I didn't flinch, but I felt like something in me died. Could they even do that? They later released me, but I knew it was only a matter of time.

"That's it," I said. "No more illegal activity for me."

I went on with my life for a couple of months before they made good on their threat. That arrest was just a prelude to the big roundup they had planned.

On the morning before Thanksgiving, the doorbell rang around eight o'clock. Catina went to the door and saw about five officers through the front window.

"Open up," they said, holding up their badges so she could see them. "Police."

Catina, partially dressed, was wearing a white ServiceMaster polo. By this time, she had worked her way up to manager. I was pleased to be able to employ several of my children, and she'd always been a hard worker. I was still asleep in the back bedroom when she opened the door to the officers.

"We have an arrest warrant for Alice Johnson," a police officer said.

Catina, shocked, allowed them further entry into the house. They had a drug-sniffing dog with them on a leash. "And another for Catina Johnson," he continued.

Catina, who doesn't normally use profanity, let one slip at hearing these words. "On what grounds?" She sat down on the couch. "I'm sitting up in here as a criminal justice major. I *know* I'm not going to jail."

"We have a witness who saw you watching another person pack a car full of cocaine," the officer said. "You have the right to remain silent—" he began.

"Packing cocaine?" she said, not believing her ears. "I can't do this without some clothes on." An officer accompanied her to her bedroom so she could finish getting dressed. In the meantime, the dog went over every part of our house, sniffing every nook and cranny. "It's not going to find anything," she said.

When I walked out from the bedroom, I couldn't believe my eyes. The police were putting shackles on my daughter's wrists, on her waist, and on her feet. Oh, they were putting them on me too, but I didn't care about that. I cared only that they were doing this to Catina.

"I know I'm not going to jail," Catina said over and over. "I haven't done anything, and if you don't do anything, you don't go to jail." Her criminal justice classes had taught her that innocent people have nothing to worry about in the American justice system. I tried to make eye contact with her, but she seemed to be in shock. "I am *not* going to jail today."

She and I didn't even talk as all of this was happening. The police led us to a van sitting in our driveway. I wondered if my neighbors were watching from their kitchen sinks as we climbed in. The police had told me they would arrest Catina, but I didn't believe they'd arrest an innocent American. Was this an intimidation tactic? They couldn't just make things up, could they? As we got settled in the van, Catina looked at me and said, "I guess I *am* going to jail today."

We drove to the federal building, where they took us to the bottom floor to get our pictures for the mug shots. Catina hadn't had time to get ready that morning, so she wasn't prepared to leave the house in such a hurry. She was on her cycle.

"Can I have some pads, please?" she asked a female officer. Her hair was in a ponytail and she wasn't wearing makeup. Of course, a mug shot is not a glamour shot, but these are the things that went through my head as an antidote to the chaos. Basic thoughts. Common thoughts. We had to be strip-searched. This was really uncomfortable for Catina because of her period. As she was humiliated, I had to deal with the fact that she was there because of me.

"Ladies, you are supposed to be in here for a seventy-two-hour holding," the officer said. "But since Thanksgiving is Thursday, you're going to have to stay until Monday."

He shut the door behind us. It was a small cell with a low wall. Catina took the pads that the officers had given her, and she had to take care of her cycle right there in front of everyone. Since no federal correctional facility existed near us that accommodated women, we had to be transferred to 201 Poplar, the Shelby County jail, which at the time took females. They shackled us again, led us out into the hall, and stopped us in front of the elevator.

"Turn around," barked an officer, though I didn't understand. I'd ridden in elevators my whole life, and I'd never seen anyone put their backs to the exit.

"Mama, turn around," Catina said, jerking me back to reality. I was in a haze. I couldn't believe they'd arrested my daughter. I turned my back to the doors and stood as the elevator jilted downward. Now that I think about it, I realize this was to prevent us from trying to make a run for it when the doors opened.

I shuffled out of the elevator and climbed into the prison van outside. We were processed into the new jail, and I was put into a bottom-floor cell with Catina.

"What is going on?" she asked.

"I guess I should come clean," I whispered. In that cell, we had one of those mother-daughter conversations I never thought I'd have. I had to tell my daughter that I had made some mistakes—big mistakes—and that I was so sorry the police had dragged her into this. Though she was sympathetic over my situation, she felt confident in her own.

"I want to see what they carved out on me," Catina said. "Because my schedule is set. I can provide a hundred witnesses on any given day who could place me far away from any cocaine van." She was in criminal justice mode, but I was so devastated I could barely process what she was saying.

Eventually we were told that the "cocaine loading" the officers had accused her of was supposed to have happened on August 16. When she heard that date, her face lit up. "August 15 is my birthday," she said. "Remember how mad I was at you," she said to me. "You made me go to Tennessee State University, so I was in Nashville registering for classes the week I wanted to party the most with my friends in Memphis."

She was so giddy that the date lined up perfectly with her clear alibi that she almost laughed. "I can't be in Nashville and Memphis at the same time. Since I had to show my ID to sign up for classes, I can prove my whereabouts. Plus, I moved into the dorm that week. My roommates can vouch for me too." She laughed and spoke into the air, as if she were talking to the deputies. "Come on with it," she said. "I got my stuff lined up right here."

In spite of her confidence, I had a growing sense of dread.

Somehow we managed to fall asleep that night, only to wake up on Thanksgiving Day in a Shelby County jail. Thanksgiving was always a big day for our family. We usually slaughtered about three hogs, and my mother made so many pies she could feed the whole town. On that day, they served us cold bologna sandwiches and sugarless Kool-Aid.

"I'm not eating this," Catina said.

"We're going to be in here for a while."

"I'd rather starve." She pushed away the food and was hungry the entire time. I ate, but my stomach churned from anxiety. Being behind bars without having the ability to leave made me feel like a caged animal.

"You're going to wear out the floor," Catina said as she eyed me pacing back and forth.

After a couple of days, they came and announced we were being transferred up to the third floor. "You first." The guard pointed to me. When they opened the door and led me out, Catina, who'd been rock solid, burst into tears. She lay down on the bunk bed in a fetal position and just bawled. Now, this girl doesn't cry. It tore me open, but I had no choice but to leave.

Eventually, they moved her upstairs too. I say "eventually," but it was probably only an hour. The guard walked her up to my new cell and said to her, "Okay, crybaby, I did what you asked. I took you to mama."

Catina rushed into the cell and embraced me. But as soon as we were reunited, an ear-piercing scream rang throughout the floor. We soon learned that a prisoner the guards nicknamed "the Wolf" lived on this floor. Actually, their nickname for her was Wolf-related but much more crass. Because of her mental issues, she screamed and screamed, all day. Then, when the guards went to check on her, she'd pee on herself and sling excrement at them.

"Just breathe, Mama," Catina said when she saw my obvious distress.

"How do people live like this?" I asked her. "Behind bars. And for six days?" I couldn't even imagine.

The days passed slowly. I taught Catina how to play dominoes, which was about the only thing we had to do to pass the time. My family came to visit. They'd been alerted that we'd been arrested, but they'd also seen it on the news. They were completely baffled that I had been involved in any criminal activity. After all, my house was always open to them. I would frequently cook for my family members, who would sometimes drop by unannounced. I never said to them, "Today isn't a good day for a visit." So when they saw on the news that my house was supposed to be Grand Central for Memphis's drug supply, they were shocked.

The first visit was the hardest. In the county jail, the visits were behind glass and we had to pick up a phone to talk. My older sister Celestine walked in, her eyes wide. My family didn't normally visit people in a jail, so they didn't know to leave their coats and purses in the car. My older sister Coria, however, knew her way around, because she had been a police officer in Memphis since 1973. When she showed up, she talked to the other officers like the old friends they were. I savored every minute of their half-hour, upbeat visit. We all assumed this was an unfortunate event that would soon blow over.

After six days, we went to court for the bail hearing. The magistrate judge announced my supposedly drug-packing daughter was being released on a $250 unsecured bail.

"And yours, Alice Johnson," he said, looking directly at me, "is $10,000." My attorney was a big guy named Wayne Emmons. He had been a Church of Christ preacher for fifteen years before becoming an attorney. He had grayish-white straight hair and a beard like Santa Claus. He wore wire-framed glasses and always had a bemused look on his face.

"The fact that they set your bail so low indicates they realize you're not a flight risk or a big fish," he explained to me. "You'll only have to pay $1,000." When I learned that others who'd been arrested were held without bail, I felt at least like the charges against me were less serious.

"But if you fail to show up for court," Wayne warned, "you'll owe all of it."

When I posted bail and got out of jail, I relished my freedom. I poured myself into my ServiceMaster company, and I spent a great deal of time developing clients and expanding my base. Owning my own business gave me something productive to think about that had nothing to do with my impending trial. I didn't want to go home and sit in the stillness of my thoughts. So I worked harder than I'd ever worked before. I always took comfort in the Bible, and my recent hardships made me rely on it even more. When I came home at night, I laid my head on the pillow and lived on Psalm 35, particularly these two verses: "Let not them that are mine enemies wrongfully rejoice over me: neither let them wink with the eye that hate me without a cause," I recited. And then, "Lord, how long wilt thou look on? Rescue my soul from their destructions, my darling from the lions."

But instead of saying the words "my darling," I would change it to "my Catina."

Rescue my Catina from the lions. I was about to break. I'd thought the officers had been bluffing. But now that they'd actually gone and arrested her, I knew they weren't playing around. This was real. I decided to cooperate fully, as long as they let her go.

"You're doing what?" Catina asked me, her head cocked to the side. We were driving to report to our probation officers, where we had to take our monthly urine test.

"I want to get you out of all this."

"Don't give in," she said. "They're bullies. I haven't done anything. I'm not afraid."

Catina had already told her defense attorney about her airtight evidence during the week they claimed she'd helped people load drugs in Memphis. Her attorney never advised her to take a deal or accept any offers, but I wasn't so sure. I knew she had zero involvement in my crime, but would this even matter to the feds? I was seriously considering throwing in the towel so I could save Catina, but she convinced me to mull it over some more.

My children were my life, and the shock of my arrest had affected everyone. My oldest son, Charles, a senior in high school, dropped out of school because he couldn't take the pressure. During this time, I encouraged him to go ahead and earn his GED and sign up for college at Tennessee State University in Nashville. And

Bryant, still haunted by his brother's death, had—unbeknownst to me—started smoking marijuana. How would they handle the additional pressure of a trial?

During this time, my partners in the ServiceMaster business were circling like vultures. Since I owned 51 percent of the enterprise, they met with me and lowballed an offer. I politely refused, since my business was exploding. That's when I hired two attorneys named Hank Shelton and Percy Harvey from the law firm of Evan, Petrie, and Cobb to help me dissolve my professional relationship with these partners, whom I thought were trying to take advantage of the situation.

Just as we were gearing up for our criminal proceedings, the nation's attention turned toward the possible criminal proceedings of one of the most famous Americans. On Friday, June 17, 1994, I was standing in my house, looking at the television. I watched the screen, which showed a white Bronco barreling down Southern California's famous freeway system with an army of squad cars in hot pursuit. News helicopters hovered above the vehicle, nimbly keeping up with the Bronco.

"What's going on?" I asked.

"That's OJ," Charles said.

"As in Simpson?" I asked, incredulous. Perhaps more than any other celebrity, he had captured the imagination and respect of almost everybody in the nation.

"They think he killed his ex-wife and her friend," he explained.

During the two years I waited for my trial after my arrest, America was transfixed by the OJ Simpson trial. Me especially. Judge Lance Ito made history by allowing this court drama to be filmed and broadcast, and I watched all I could. I had been accused of a crime, and I wanted to learn everything I could about what a trial might be like for me. I'd seen courtroom dramas and dramatizations on TV, but this was the first time I'd been able to see an actual court case unfold in real time.

You couldn't turn on the television without seeing the main players there on the screen, and the people involved in it became household names. Marsha Clark was the star prosecutor, and America obsessed over her hair, makeup, and general manner. Kato Kaelin was a memorable, sandy-haired witness from the trial. Mark Fuhrman was the investigator who found the notorious bloody glove. On the defense side, OJ's trial lawyers were dubbed the "Dream Team." They included Johnnie Cochran, who coined the snappy "If the glove doesn't fit, you must acquit"; Alan Dershowitz, a high-profile appellate adviser for the defense team; and of course OJ's old personal friend and defense attorney Robert Kardashian.

On October 3, 1995, the OJ Simpson nonguilty verdict was watched live by approximately 150 million people, which made it one of the most watched events in television history. After watching this high-profile case that had been opened up for public consumption, I more fully understood the stakes of what my daughter and I were up against.

This better understanding scared me to my core. I cried out to God in prayer. "Lord, whatever you have for me, I'll do it as long as you release Catina." She had gotten pregnant, and I didn't want her to have one ounce of extra stress. I sank to a new low when they finally set a trial date. I'd decided to just quit fighting all this. My daughter had to be my priority.

Catina was still confident, but she didn't understand the possible ramifications. The Anti-Drug Abuse Act had been amended in 1988 to add conspiracy to its list of offenses. Technically, anyone who knows about criminal activity and participates in it can be called a conspirator. Almost half the women in prison at the time, under those mandatory minimum sentences, were convicted of conspiracy.[1] Would the jury look at me and see a drug conspirator? I wasn't stashing money in an overseas account or in a mattress anywhere. Though my business was finally getting off the ground, I was barely able to make ends meet.

Before the trial date, the public defender called and told us the charges against Catina had been dropped. No one told us why they dropped the charges, but I assume it was because they had no real evidence against Catina. If prosecutors were using Catina's arrest as a bargaining tool, it wasn't working. They probably figured that if I hadn't budged in all that time, I probably wouldn't ever budge. They had no idea that if they had waited just one day later, I would've given them whatever they wanted.

◇◇◇◇◇◇◇◇◇◇

To be specific, I was accused of participating in a drug conspiracy. The charges against me sounded scary and legitimate. I was charged with "attempted" possession of drugs (not possession), money laundering (a charge that automatically came with the drug charge), and money structuring (a charge that resulted from

---

[1] David France, "You Be the Jury: Does This Woman Deserve to Be Locked Up for 24 Years?," *Glamour*, June 1999, available at http://www.hr95.org/glamour.htm.

how I purchased my home even though it had no connection to my work with Ted).

Since I knew I had not done all that, their complete overreach caused me to shudder, but it also emboldened me. I had committed a crime by passing along messages as a "telephone mule," but I wasn't a drug dealer. I figured I wouldn't be charged. When the government offered an unofficial plea bargain for cooperation—three to five years in a camp—I balked. A camp is a small, minimum-security facility on the same grounds, but outside the security fence. Still. Three years in prison? Six days in that Shelby County jail had almost done me in. Plus, Wayne advised me not to take it. "Their case is weak," he said. "You don't want this on your record for the rest of your life."

So, after two years of being on bond, my trial date was set.

Hank Shelton, my attorney in the ServiceMaster case, asked me about my upcoming trial. "Who's your judge?"

"Julia Gibbons," I responded.

"You won't be going to trial on Monday," he said, shaking his head. "Her husband works here at my firm. His name is even on our letterhead. It raises questions of conflict of interest." He knew I'd paid at least $20,000 to his firm. Even though the judge's husband didn't do work on my ServiceMaster case, I didn't like the connection between my civil case and criminal case.

But when Wayne asked Judge Gibbons to recuse herself, she was dismissive. She explained that her husband's firm's association with me was nobody's concern. She believed it was not prohibited by ethical rules and explained she didn't discuss his business with him.

"You know I'm not accusing Your Honor," Wayne said, trying to pacify her. It was almost as if he was trying to impress her instead of demanding that she do the right thing. Whatever the strategy, it didn't work. She denied our request for recusal.

I didn't know this at the time, but Wayne had needed to file an official motion to cause her to recuse herself. Since he didn't do this, the trial plunged ahead. It was the first red flag of many that would make me doubt whether Wayne had my best interest at heart.

In September 1996, my trial finally began.

Chapter 6

⌐∿⌐

I stood accused.

Thankfully, the Constitution of the United States guarantees the right of a citizen to a fair and impartial trial. Maybe I was naive, but this guarantee gave me certain expectations: I expected that my judge would be fair and impartial; I expected the prosecutor to fight fairly; I expected to be tried by a jury of my peers, selected according to the laws of the land; I expected to be represented by competent and loyal counsel; I expected to be considered innocent until proven guilty.

Sixteen people were indicted. Four of us went to trial, three of us women and one man. I was accused of being involved in a Houston–Memphis drug operation. The government charged us with cocaine conspiracy and money laundering, and claimed our actions involved at least $1 million, which we had hidden away in secret compartments in customized "load cars" such as station wagons. These cars were then exchanged for tar buckets packed to the rim with cocaine.

They portrayed me as a main leader of a drug ring they claimed imported two to three thousand kilograms of cocaine into our community. Now, I knew I'd been wrong to pass along information from one drug dealer to the next, but I definitely wasn't who they were making me out to be. Hearing their accusations, I was astounded, especially since I had no idea where they'd come up with those high numbers. At the time, prosecutors could attribute something called "ghost dope" to us in our trial. "Ghost dope" was the phrase defense attorneys used to describe drug quantities based on the testimony of cooperating witnesses in an alleged conspiracy even if those drugs were never actually recovered. Prosecutors were also allowed to assign the entire amount of alleged drug weight in a drug operation to a single defendant (including ghost dope), even if that defendant played a relatively minor role in the alleged conspiracy. As a result, the prosecutors in my case estimated that we'd moved thousands of kilos of cocaine, even though they had recovered nowhere near that amount from cooperating witnesses. "Ghost dope" was an accurate nickname, because it would come back to haunt me at sentencing.

The prosecutor Stuart Canale had an ace in the hole, one which had been in the newspapers building up to the trial. In discovery, he received testimony from one of Memphis's most prominent sons, who was willing to tie me to a drug dealer. Michael Wilson, a former basketball star at the University of Memphis, had a fifty-five-inch vertical leap, which earned him the nickname "Wild Thing." (Later, the six-foot-five player set a world record by dunking on a twelve-foot goal.) He enjoyed a good amount of popularity in Memphis and had just signed a contract with the Harlem Globetrotters. He was also friends with my older sister Celestine's youngest child, Bernard. In 1994, Bernard was drafted to the Philadelphia Eagles as one of the NFL's first-round draft picks. To celebrate, we attended a huge party at a ballroom at a Memphis hotel. I'll never forget that night. We ate a Philadelphia Eagles cake with our family members, local politicians, business owners, police officers, and many of Bernard's friends. A photographer was there, taking photos of every table, to make sure we never forgot that festive night. One of my favorite photographs was of my mom, sisters, and me sitting at a table, having the best time. My head was thrown so far back in laughter that the photograph caught my secret gold tooth. Wilson was there too, and the prosecutor was going to use this party as evidence against me.

How? In his opening statements, Stuart Canale told the jurors that Wilson was going to testify about my involvement with Maurice Mondie, whom Wilson had brought as his guest to the party. Mondie was a drug dealer and listed on my indictment, so the prosecution used two photos taken at this party. One showed Mondie and Wilson at a table. Another showed some friends and me. They didn't use the other hundreds of photos taken—of my family, the police officers, and city officials—so that the jury had the impression that this was a "drug party."

I didn't know everyone at that party, but I'm assuming since I spent most of the evening with my mama and family members (including my sister, who was a police officer) that I wasn't accidentally hanging out with drug dealers. It was preposterous, but the accusation worried me. Especially since the jurors would have an unusual amount of reverence for Wilson, an athlete who'd made it big from our city.

The prosecution trotted out confessed drug dealers I'd never seen before. Facing maximum sentencing, they'd been given a deal by the feds that they couldn't refuse. I didn't know this at the time, but whenever someone is up on drug charges, cooperating witnesses frequently jump in on that case to reduce their own sentences. Suddenly, the formerly tight-lipped dealers were very talkative, and it was almost like a competition to see how creative and elaborate the stories about me could possibly be. The more they talked, the better their deal. Because information is valuable, they concocted a lot of it.

My defense attorneys attempted to discredit these drug dealers, calling them "a parade of liars who would sell out their own mothers for thirty pieces of silver." Also, one of the attorneys said, "This case is more fascinating than any novel you've ever read. The government took the keys to the prison door and said, 'If you want to stay out of prison, you have to help us get our target.'" He dramatically held up his keys and jingled them, acting as if the government were dangling the keys to the prison in front of the drug dealers, enticing them to fabricate their testimony. And that was exactly right.

One drug dealer in particular made outrageous claims: that I was one of the two ringleaders in Memphis. I couldn't believe my ears. I'd been called many things in my life, but no one had ever called me a kingpin. As the man was on the stand, claiming to know me well, I noticed his eyes were actually not on me. I watched him talk, and . . . was it possible? Yes, he was looking at my codefendant. I had an idea.

My mother, Sallie Mae Boggan, was a woman before her time. She was a fantastic cook, a civil rights advocate, a woman of God, and my hero.

My father, Raymond Boggan, worked hard to provide for his family. He was a praying man who loved his wife and children.

My siblings and I survived the 1970s, but the tumult of the era shaped the direction of my life for years to come.

By the time I was sixteen, I was already a mother and a wife. This photo shows me with my firstborn daughter, Tretessa; my siblings; and my niece and nephew.

My 1973 yearbook photo from Olive Branch High School. I was educated at East Side High School until integration occurred in 1970, and while integration was important, my education at East Side was fantastic! We had great black teachers, a talented black band, and we had some great achievers who came out of our little school.

Cory, aka Coco, was a good son who always wanted to quietly do what was right. I was proud to learn that he had gotten baptized before his tragic death.

My oldest sister, Lena (deceased), and her firstborn, Jeannette. Mama assigned Lena to help dress me for church. She had her work cut out for her because I never sat still to get my hair combed!

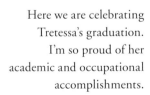

My children loved celebrating birthdays. Especially eating the ice cream and cake!

Here we are celebrating Tretessa's graduation. I'm so proud of her academic and occupational accomplishments.

My sister Celestine died while I was in prison. Even though we were fourteen years apart, I felt like I could tell her anything.

I always enjoy spending evenings with my family.

I love this photo, because it shows us laughing at an NFL party celebrating my nephew signing with the Philadelphia Eagles. Not only does it show the joy of the moment, but it also shows my "secret" gold tooth–one that the prison would later take from me.

My parents celebrated their fiftieth wedding anniversary with their children. Their marriage was always an inspiration for me, a solid basis for our tight-knit family.

My sister Thelma and I pose for a photo in prison at Dublin, located in California. Though the walls did have razor wire, FCI Dublin had more green spaces and flowers than I expected.

My sisters and I have always been super close. This photo pictures Dolores, Thelma, Coria, me, Patricia, and Ruby during a sisters-only prison visit.

In prison, a strong faith helped me survive through the hard times. I was a part of the Jubilee Praise Dancers at Carswell, pictured here in 1999.

My daughter Tretessa was able to visit me more frequently than the rest of my family members, because the distance to the first two prisons was very great. This photo shows a visit she made to Carswell in 1999.

In 2004, I enjoyed a meaningful visit from my children. *From left to right:* Bryant, Catina, me, Tretessa, and Charles.

I always tried to make holidays special in the prisons, since the women sometimes got sad that they couldn't celebrate with their loved ones. I put on uplifting holiday-related programs and decorated the chapel to make them feel like they weren't in prison at all. This photo shows me celebrating Christmas at Carswell.

My grandchildren visiting me for the first time in prison. *Left to right:* Justin, me, Shelby, and Kashea.

Two of my sisters and my brother visited me at Carswell. I appreciated all the effort they went to in order to put a smile on my face.

One friend I had at Carswell was Sharanda Jones (*left*). We gravitated toward each other because we were both first-time, nonviolent offenders who had life sentences—and we both loved to laugh. She had been at the prison for a while before we got close. Eventually, she was granted clemency by President Obama.

A creative group who participated in the plays I wrote in prison! *Left to right:* Cristie, Stacey, me, and Takisha.

I was always ready for Christmas. This photo shows me with my dear friend Chanel Jones. She and I used to walk around the exercise track every day to stay in shape.

In 2014, my friends and I had fun pretending that I'd just gotten clemency. But I was left behind. *Left to right:* Fifty (really named Barbara Turner), me, Paula, and Patty.

I desperately missed Tretessa, Catina, and my granddaughters, Shelby and Kashea, so I appreciated them visiting me in prison. When this photo was taken, I had already been denied clemency twice.

Prison restrictions for visitation were sometimes hard to understand and follow. This photo shows my nephew JT, Patricia, and Jasmine visiting in Aliceville. I remember that JT had to go buy new clothes at Fred's, because the khakis he'd worn weren't allowed for some reason.

This photo shows me and my friend Fifty. Fifty was also a lifer, like me, and a very gifted artist. We worked on every play and project together at Aliceville.

Dolores and my brother-in-law Reginald visited me in Aliceville. Being closer to my family was a dream come true.

I was proud of the fact that I graduated from Electrical while I was at Aliceville. I always believed in bettering myself, even though the government told me I never had chance at living as a free woman.

Rubies for Life is a Christian, faith-based program offered while I was at Aliceville. This photo shows my graduation ceremony.

Warden Washington-Aducci and life coach Sandy Lewis presented me with the Rubies for Life diploma.

I loved writing and performing skits in prison. This photo shows me acting in a skit I wrote called *Bullying, It's Just Not Fun*, at a children's event in Aliceville.

My daughters, Tretessa and Catina, fought for my return at the White House in 2016.

Here I am talking at a #Cut50 event via video while I was in prison.

This photo shows Patricia, Dolores, and Thelma in Washington, DC, in front of the Department of Justice in 2016.

This photo shows Catina and me just moments after I walked out of prison. I'll never forget that feeling of true elation.

My reunion with my grandson after twenty-one years. The last time I saw my oldest grandson, he was only eighteen months old.

On the day of my release, I greeted Kendall Ciesemier—the MIC reporter who interviewed me for the video that Kim Kardashian West came across in her Twitter feed.

This photo shows the attorneys Kim Kardashian West assembled to help save my life. *From left to right:* Jennifer Turner, Brittany Barnett, Shawn Holley, Mike Schooll, and Jake Horowitz with MIC. I will always appreciate their hard work and dedication.

The first time I was able to hold my grandtwins, Amira and Aiden, was a powerfully emotional moment. Up until this point, I'd only seen them on video chat.

Bryant, Shontoria, Catina, Xavier, me, Charles, Christopher, and Tretessa celebrate the Fourth of July. My first holiday at home—I was feeling very patriotic on this day!

This photo shows my children and two sisters arriving at Google. My son Charles, second on the right, is now a firefighter—ironically, he set my hair on fire as a toddler!

Me with some of the advocates who helped fight for my freedom. *Left to right:* Topeka Sam, Brittany Barnett, me, Jennifer Turner, Amy Povah, and Nkechi Taifa.

This photo shows me at a Prison Fellowship event honoring Mark Holden, Koch's lead attorney who helms a coalition to fight the tragic results of overcriminalization.

Onstage at a Google fireside chat about criminal justice reform with Kim Kardashian West and Malika Saar.

After I bragged about my Southern cooking to Kim, she asked me to cook with her during a visit to California. I showed Kim how to make biscuits from scratch, the easy way. We also made beef and gravy, fried chicken, cream potatoes, baked macaroni, collard greens, and much more. I got to meet Kanye and eat with both of them, as well as Kim's sisters, her mother, and her children. Even some of her extended family members—nieces and nephews—came to meet me.

This photo shows me, Kim Kardashian West, Van Jones, and Louis Reed in Los Angeles, on November 14, 2018—the day that President Donald Trump announced he was endorsing the First Step Act.

On the day of the State of the Union Address, I went to the White House for the first time. This photograph was taken in the Oval Office with me, President Trump, Patricia, and Dolores.

Official White House photo by Shealah Craighead

"He doesn't even know who I am," I whispered to Wayne. "Have him point me out."

Wayne rose to his feet to address this man. "Can you come down and point out Alice Marie Johnson?"

Confidently, the man stepped down from the witness stand, swaggered over to where the defendants were sitting, and—with a flourish—pointed to my codefendant. He dramatically said, "That's Alice." The jury and the courtroom erupted in laughter, and it took a few moments before everybody settled back down.

Another drug dealer was the prosecution's star witness. Ramon Ramirez, known as Rambo, was facing a life sentence, which could magically be reduced through cooperation. Though none of the other people said they brought drugs to my house—why would they?—Ramirez claimed he'd been to my house over twenty times. I don't know about you, but if I have been to a place over twenty times, you better believe I know how to get there. I might even know a few shortcuts. And so, I had an idea that could reveal Ramirez for the liar that he was. To show that his claim couldn't be true, I went to Kinko's and enlarged a map of the Memphis area big enough to place on an easel.

In his cross-examination, Wayne placed the map before the court and made a request to Ramirez. "Show the jury how to get to Alice Marie Johnson's house," he said. When Ramirez stepped down from the witness stand, his hands were shaking so bad. He had no idea where to begin. He stuck out his index finger and made a zigzag pattern across the map. By the time he stopped his finger, he'd landed on an area across the river.

"There," he said, pointing to the Mississippi-Arkansas Bridge.

I lived in the opposite direction, nowhere near that bridge. Somehow, though he'd covered much of that map with his shaking finger, he'd totally missed my area.

"No," Wayne said. "That is not where Alice Marie Johnson lives. But I can see that it might be difficult. Try again." This time, Ramirez pointed to another completely incorrect area. Over and over, he failed to locate the house he'd supposedly gone to so many times. Eventually Wayne ended his misery and revealed that the location of my house was in a totally different area. The courtroom, once again, burst into laughter.

It wasn't just these drug dealers who made the prosecution's case look thin. I certainly took note when their "star" witness Michael Wilson failed to take the stand.

I'd actually been very prepared for his testimony as I knew the allegations he was making against me quite well. Wayne had had two years to conduct appropriate pretrial investigation, to look at discovery and prepare a strategy. But he frequently asked me to consider the evidence and come back the next day with a list of questions I thought he should ask. I never went to law school, yet I was calling all the shots. Wayne seemed to think this was some sort of improv performance. (Regrettably, this is closer to the truth than I realized at the time. Years after he blew my case, Wayne quit the practice of law to become a comedian. Yes, really.)

One evening I settled down with a stack of evidence, curious about what Michael Wilson's role in this trial was. Looking through everything, I learned that Wilson tied me to drug dealers and even claimed to have seen me at a restaurant with Ted, along with a suspicious-looking man. I flopped back into the couch and let myself sink into the cushions. I remembered seeing Wilson one day when I was having dinner with a friend—not Ted—and his brother.

I'd spotted Wilson across the way, and pointed him out to my friend's brother, the way you do when you see someone prominent. He was a fun-loving guy, the type of person who'd appreciate seeing a future Harlem Globetrotter. Hardly suspicious.

We didn't go over and speak. Wilson was just an eighteen-year-old, and I wasn't confident that he would want to have his meal interrupted by his friend's aunt. But as Wilson was leaving the restaurant, he passed our table.

"Hey, Michael," I said. "Someone wants to meet you." Part of me enjoyed being able to call him by his first name and get this introduction.

That's all that happened. I'd seen him at a restaurant, while I was with my friend and his brother.

Because I remembered this event so clearly, I was ready to counter Wilson's version, but on the day he was supposed to appear in court, he wasn't called. And not only was he not called that day, he was never called in the trial at all for reasons totally unknown to me. I was shocked, especially since he'd seemingly been such an important part not just of the prosecution's opening statement but of their initial indictment against me, an indictment based in part on information from Wilson. In addition, the jurors had already been told that Wilson was going to testify and play an important role. He was a celebrity, a recognizable name that they teased and then removed without explanation. No one questioned why his testimony was pulled. Surely this was a cause for a mistrial, I thought. Yet the trial continued.

Perhaps it was because of surprises like this that the prosecutors continued to rely on visual aids to convict me in the eyes of the jury. Even though my conviction was largely based on dope attributable to my alleged coconspirators as well as ghost dope, it didn't stop the prosecutor from coming in one day with bricks and bricks of the stuff, plopping them down on a table for the jury to see.

"Twenty-five thousand dollars for this piece of garbage," prosecutor Stuart Canale said as he dramatically held up a brick of compressed cocaine wrapped in brown plastic. I couldn't believe my eyes. *So that's what a brick of cocaine looks like when it's not on television*, I thought. I figured Wayne would object. The jury would no doubt assume these were drugs taken from my house. "That's what this is about," Canale said. "Money."

Though there were certainly dramatic moments, the trial wasn't what I expected after watching *Perry Mason*. These were some of the most important six weeks of my life, yet the people involved were not even paying attention to critical details.

For example, one juror would sleep during huge portions of testimony. He didn't doze off and try to hide it, like a student in school who can't resist getting some shut-eye. No, this juror brought a sleep mask to the court proceedings, threw his head back, and conked out while testimony was being given. When the defense went forward to make our case, the juror turned his back toward us. When one of the attorneys brought this to the judge's attention, to her credit, she did tell him he couldn't wear that sleep mask anymore, and she even admonished him to wear shoes and to quit propping his feet up during the trial. His behavior was inappropriate for a fast food restaurant, let alone a court proceeding.

The judge allowed the jury to view exhibits on breaks, over lunch, and in the mornings, as long as they did not discuss the case among themselves or with anyone else. (She gave these explicit instructions three times.) Yet on October 22, one of the jurors, who happened to be pregnant, came forward and revealed that everyone had been chatting.

"I don't know if it's important," she said. "But yesterday it was mentioned that a party was given for Alice Marie Johnson's nephew. Well, I'm friends with her nephew and niece. When I mentioned this, they laughed and made jokes, asking me if I had been invited to that drug party."

The judge dismissed this juror, but not the others, who had violated her instructions even more egregiously. The entire jury panel was tainted, and a mistrial should've been declared, but it wasn't.

Another juror-related mistake was that one of them should've been excused after hiding the close family relationship between her husband and one of the arresting officers, but she wasn't. Though Judge Gibbons failed to dismiss white jurors who had just cause for dismissal, she did dismiss two black jurors. When a white juror lacked transportation to court, the court provided transportation. When a black juror lacked transportation, the court made no special arrangements.

The government wanted the jury to believe I had orchestrated the movement of cocaine from a Colombian drug cartel into Memphis. As a "drug information mule," I frequently talked to strangers on the phone, but my only knowledge of cartels came from television and the movies. Honestly, I didn't watch many shows like that. The prosecutors, however, believed they had iron-clad evidence that I had talked to the cartel: a phone call that came from Colombia to my home.

I saw the phone number, which had the Colombian nation code. I didn't recognize it but had no reason to believe the records were wrong. Dread started to grow in my stomach.

A conversation had obviously happened, but something didn't add up.

Unless this agent had recorded the call or had ESP, he couldn't have surmised who was on the other end of the line. I knew it was not me, but I didn't know how to combat his argument. As I stared at the number, I noticed the date beside the call: October 2.

The day my son was killed.

Suddenly I understood what had happened.

I was so bereft over losing Coco, the hospital had given me sedatives to calm me down. My family reported that the phone was ringing off the hook while I was at the hospital, loved ones trying to determine the status of Coco. I remembered specifically that they'd told me my cousin, who was living in Colombia after she got married, had called to find out more information about the tragedy.

The call had happened, but it was about my son's death, not drugs.

The call had happened, but I didn't even answer it.

Thankfully, I could provide evidence to prove this. I brought in my son's obituary and the prescription for my sedatives, which was dated October 2.

When Wayne attempted to submit these as evidence, the prosecutor objected. "They're simply trying to play on the pity of the jury. The fact that her son died has no bearing."

"Sustained," Judge Gibbons said.

Something about this accusation, the objection, and the ruling felt particularly evil. It was devastating that I had to bring up the death of my son in such a context, when I could barely even speak his name. And all my efforts came to nothing. The jury didn't hear my side, and they were left with the impression that the family members calling to find out about Coco's death were really members of a Colombian drug cartel.

With a sinking feeling, I realized there was nothing I could do to change their minds.

◇◇◇◇◇◇◇◇◇◇

I was scared.

I'd pleaded "not guilty" as a legal maneuver, but I knew deep down I was guilty of breaking the law. I'd taken a shortcut, I'd tried to get money fast, I'd closed my eyes to the evil of drugs. Regardless of the details—or even the outcome of this trial—any role I played involving drugs was inexcusable, wrong, and illegal. I wanted desperately to get out of this mess, but I'd done too much and gone too far. I couldn't turn back the clock.

Though I'd lost confidence in Wayne, now was the time to put on my best defense. The prosecution had rested, so I took a deep breath and steeled my nerves for this—the most important— portion of the trial.

The prosecutor claimed I had no legitimate source of income, so I was therefore living off my drug-related activities. To combat this narrative, I wanted to show that my ServiceMaster company was creating enough income to pay the bills, and I used any extra money it brought to invest back into the company. When I'd tried to submit my financial records into evidence during my testimony, the prosecutor objected. The judge sustained the objection, saying my money had nothing to do with the trial.

However, if I was a drug kingpin, I was one of the worst. This drug operation was supposedly worth $2.5 million, but my lifestyle didn't reflect that. Though some of my codefendants had nice cars and houses, my house payment was less than $900 for a home worth less than $100,000. I didn't even own my car free and clear. My mother took the stand and testified that she had to give me money to pay my legal fees. That should've embarrassed me. But what hurt more was seeing my mama up there in the witness box being questioned about the failures of one of her children.

My family members and other witnesses were also called to testify. Unanimously, they said they'd never seen any odd or illegal activity at my house, even though they frequently dropped by unannounced. Also, the police talked to my neighbors, and none of them were called to testify at my trial. I knew why: undoubtedly they testified that they'd seen nothing, because there was nothing to see.

When another witness took the stand, he recounted the actions of a certain Memphis police officer named Mark Chisholm. But during his testimony, he seemingly got confused. He stated that the man's name was Mark Fuhrman, before correcting himself. Fuhrman, of course, was the Los Angeles Police Department detective who'd become famous for his part in the OJ Simpson murder case and famous for his use of racist language against black people.

That was all I needed. Was the witness trying to be funny? If so, I think it had the opposite effect. I think it made the white jurors uncomfortable. Regardless, the jurors were suddenly reminded of the racially charged Simpson case, which had just concluded. Would the jury attempt to make the OJ verdict right by convicting the black defendant before them?

This didn't seem to be going well. It was obvious that Wayne was giving a half-hearted defense, but I didn't know exactly what else to do.

Occasionally, when I worked up the courage, I looked back and saw the worried expressions on my parents' faces. We'd all figured I would eventually escape this situation without it being too disruptive to my life. My brother, Julius, who was there sitting in the courtroom the most, always wore a sober look on his face. It was uniquely hard on my sister Coria, who was a police officer at the time and who worked in research and development on the twelfth floor of the building in which I was being tried. She couldn't come to court as often, because her presence caused a stir. She knew many of the officers involved in my case and had to endure speculation like "How much did Coria know about her sister's illegal activities?"

My defense was remarkably short, since Wayne skipped critical witnesses. I tried to convince him to call certain people, but he seemed to cover his ill preparedness with a confidence that indicated we didn't need the testimony. He said he had already impeached the testimony of their witnesses.

"We don't need a big defense," he said. "We're going to use their witnesses against them."

The trial lasted six weeks and involved testimony from over forty witnesses, more than 180 exhibits, and that ever-mysterious "ghost dope," with an estimated street value of $2.5 million. I had also been accused of moving an "estimated" amount of drugs: two to three thousand kilograms (though the people who testified didn't even testify to that much). Where in the world did these big figures come from? I had no idea. I guess if you put the word "estimated" in front, you can be careless with the amount.

During closing arguments, Wayne continued to cast aspersions on the testimony of the drug dealers. "If you had to leave your kid with somebody, would you leave him with one of these accusers or with Alice Marie Johnson?" he asked. The jurors were invited to ponder which of us seemed more honest. He continued, "That has to do with the credibility of witnesses." Then Wayne finally said something that I thought was really effective—and also had the added benefit of being true. About ten years before this, the fast food chain Wendy's had a funny commercial featuring an old lady asking a question about other chains' burgers: "Where's the beef?"

Wayne looked at the jurors and used that same catchphrase to describe the prosecution's lack of evidence. They hadn't shown that I had any money, any drugs, or any knowledge of this greater drug ring. They hadn't shown I'd touched or even seen any drugs.

"Where's the beef?" Wayne asked the jury, before pausing dramatically. He was attempting to hammer home my lack of money and possessions in his closing statements. I could only hope and pray that the jury was convinced.

The week of deliberation was incredibly tense. We heard rumors that the jury was hung. Also, when people stood outside the deliberation room, they reported hearing hollering and screaming from inside.

To be honest, it worried me. But it also worried the prosecution. In fact, they were so uncertain that they sent me a message through my attorney.

"They've indicated that they would be willing to offer you eight to ten years," Wayne said, "if you're willing to plead guilty."

"What do you think?" I asked.

"You've got a fifty-fifty chance. I'm just passing along the message," he said. "But I feel good about our chances."

"If you feel good," I said, "I feel good." Wayne let them know I wasn't interested. But the drama continued.

On the morning of October 29, a juror's house was burglarized. Since his door had not been replaced and his home was opened, he feared he couldn't concentrate on the trial. He scheduled a meeting with the judge, the only person who could excuse him from deliberations.

When he met with Judge Gibbons, he explained his situation more fully. He told her that he'd seen a man in the courtroom he knew to be a thief. Since he was obviously tied up as a juror and not at home, he wondered if this thief had targeted his house.

"Judge, I also need to tell you something else," the juror said, changing the topic. He told her that the jurors had apparently gotten anxious about getting home in time for Halloween. Apparently some of them believed that trick-or-treating was more important than my future. He told her they were "rushing" the verdict and that he wasn't sure how long he could stand his ground to demand that everyone have time to look at the evidence fairly. It seemed that the courtroom's climate of urgency about obtaining a verdict had spilled over into the minds of the jury.

Even a hint that something was wrong in the jury room should've caused the court to investigate. Though the juror did his duty reporting the matter, the judge never took further action.

Later that morning, the juror concluded that the thief in the courtroom and the home burglary was a coincidence. After his door was fixed, he told the judge he would return for deliberations.

"Can you be fair?" she asked.

"Yes," he responded.

This should've been a relief, since we had no other alternates. Yet Judge Gibbons excused him as a deliberating juror. This left only eleven jurors.

When we gathered for the verdict on October 31, 1996, we stood as the judge entered the courtroom.

"The jury finds Alice Marie Johnson"—she paused ever so dramatically—"guilty."

On Halloween, the eleven-person jury found me guilty of money laundering and participation in a cocaine conspiracy. I was handcuffed and led out of the courtroom. But as I was walking, two federal agents came up to me, put their mouths to my ear, and said, quickly, "Trick or treat," then, a little more slowly, "Trick or treat," then, with great relish, *Trick or treat!*

This obscene singsong Halloween taunt was the last thing I would hear before beginning my life of captivity.

Chapter 7

As soon as the verdict came down, I was taken into custody and sent to the jail at 201 Poplar. My first night there, I barely slept because I replayed all the events of the day. I couldn't get the faces of my family members out of my head as I watched them come to grips with the verdict.

A couple of days after my sentencing, I was alerted that I had an attorney visit. Wayne assured me that everything would turn out all right. "I just want you to know that I am immediately filing your direct appeal," he said. "I'll fight this every step of the way. I bet you'll be out in thirteen months."

"I can't do thirteen months," I said. "I could barely do six days." As it turned out, I ended up being in that county jail six months before my sentencing. While I was there, I called out to God. I discovered God always honors a cry, even from a woman like me.

I found a book on a book cart that was called *Free on the Inside.* It was actually a New International Reader's Version Bible, which meant that the language was simpler. I'd never read any-thing other than the King James version. Suddenly I could under-stand what I was reading, and a fire was lit in my spirit. I fell in love with the Word of God! Over those months in county jail, I read it from cover to cover, devouring the truths that were inside. Other women even started coming to me asking for prayer. They assumed I was religious since I was always reading the Bible. I started going to Bible studies and eventually taught Bible studies in my unit. Some people call this "jailhouse religion," but I didn't care. My faith had been reignited!

The first day of spring is a time for new beginnings. Never had that been truer than March 21, 1997, because it was the day I would be sentenced.

I'd worn attractive clothes every day to trial, in my effort to look professional. On the day of the sentencing, Catina brought me a couple of outfits that would allow me to stand with pride before the judge. However, after I selected one and began to slip it on, a guard came into the room, a look of embarrassment on her face. "I don't know what's wrong, Miss Johnson," she said, "but we received an order that you are not allowed to wear those clothes. The judge wants to see you in jail clothes."

She reluctantly handed me a folded prison uniform, clothing that reeked of shame. But the judge had another thing coming if she thought she could break me by taking away my clothes, makeup, and jewelry. I traded prison uniforms with another prisoner who'd kept hers under the mattress so it was crisp and wrinkle-free. Then I fashioned hoop earrings out of aluminum foil and used red Kool-Aid to stain my lips. I took a deep breath and rose to my full height before my transport. Under my breath, I was reciting Psalm 23. "Yea, though I walk through the valley of the shadow of death, I will fear no evil." My dignity, a gift from God, was not something a judge could take away.

When I walked into the courtroom, I glanced at my family. Everyone was trying to make eye contact with me, so I obliged by giving them a reassuring gaze. They took me over to the side of the bench, where I stood. The bailiff then announced, "All rise." Everybody in the room stood as Judge Gibbons walked in wearing black judicial robes. I stood in orange.

"Have you already reviewed your presentencing report?"

I had. They'd delivered it to me a few weeks earlier, and it scared me. Judge Gibbons had already sentenced Ted to life, whereas my other codefendent had gotten nineteen years. The confessed drug dealers had gotten seriously reduced sentences, if any at all. Since I had no rap sheet and no prior convictions, I figured I would not be treated more harshly than "Babro," "the Preacher," "Scarface," and "Rambo." When I read my presentencing report, however, to my utter shock, I saw that the recommended sentence was life. I simply put it down and didn't look at it again. I didn't even want to consider this option, nor did I even believe it was possible. Something on that paper had to be wrong. Wayne had never even remotely mentioned this as a possibility. "Yes," I responded. "I've read it."

As Judge Gibbons began to talk, she described me as the quintessential drug entrepreneur. She noted that "clearly the impact of two to three thousand kilograms of cocaine in this community is very significant," again referencing the amount of ghost dope as though it were fact. She went on to say that I ran drugs like I ran my business. My business? What did she know about my business? My pulse quickened. This information had never been introduced into the trial. The prosecutor had tried to portray my business as a failure, using that supposed lack of success as evidence that I had to be getting money from drugs.

But even though she was right about my business skills, the words still didn't make sense. I was an entrepreneur in the sense that I wanted my ServiceMaster businesses to do well, yes. But I was just an information mule, a desperate person who had gotten involved in misdeeds. I hadn't been responsible for thousands of kilograms of drugs. Judge Gibbons made me sound like El Chapo.

As I was thinking about the inaccuracy of her statement, she said the word "Life." I then heard her say, "Plus twenty-five years."

Because of the mandatory sentencing laws, Judge Gibbons had no leeway in sentencing. The crimes of which I'd been convicted carried life in prison. We could've all seen this coming, since it was in the presentencing report. But because of denial, or ignorance, or simply not understanding the criminal justice system, I only now understood the gravity of my situation. I'd entrusted my life to my legal counsel without fully understanding the stakes: that the laws around my sentence were nonnegotiable. Furthermore, there would not even be a chance for me to redeem myself at a parole hearing, because the federal system has no parole. I had just received an unexecuted sentence of death.

I let the words spread out in my head before reacting. I'll never forget the collective gasp that came from the courtroom. It was a breathy mixture of both disbelief and anguish. And after that horrible sound, nothing. Just silence, for one beat, then two. Then a sound much worse than the gasp.

Weeping.

I didn't look back at my elderly parents. I knew the sound of crying was coming from my dad, the hardworking man who'd gotten up early to milk the cows, helped us pick cotton, then secretly built a house with his own hands so we could have a better life than sharecropping. I couldn't bear to see the man who baptized me in that muddy lake sobbing. I'd seen him cry in church while praying, but this was different. Raw grief.

Next to him sat my mother, that strong woman who'd raised me on blackberry cobbler and the soaring words of Martin Luther King Jr. This was not how any of us had expected my life to turn out. I was trying to hold my tears in check, to swallow them down. I wanted to cry, to scream. I felt like my head would explode. My throat burned. But I didn't want to lose control of myself in this moment.

I would apparently have plenty of time to process this. However, I think it angered Judge Gibbons that I didn't break down and cry. She was still talking, and I forced myself to listen to her words. She was recommending I spend my life sentence at a prison in Texas called Carswell, because they had a mental health department. She looked at me unkindly and said, "You will need a mental health facility as you come to grips with your life sentence."

My head snapped up and I met her eyes. The insinuation was insulting, that I'd be so weak that I'd end up with mental health issues. *You'll lose your mind before I lose mine,* I thought.

When I was walking out with my hands cuffed, I had to pass my family. I turned to look at them and I faced them.

"It's going to be okay," I tried to tell them. I wanted them to know this was not the end—this was something I felt strongly even in that moment of chaos. On the way out the door, the court reporter Joe Moore stopped me. "Miss Johnson," he said. "It's going to be okay. You aren't going to do all that time."

I paused to look at his eyes. Why would he say such a thing at a time like this? Yet his words stuck with me.

◇◇◇◇◇◇◇◇◇◇

Women's prisons are more spread out across the nation than men's prisons, and I soon learned that I would not be going to Carswell. I wondered if Judge Gibbons had just recommended Carswell at the sentencing to insult my mental health. Instead, I would be going to a prison in California, I was devastated to learn. Even for a short visit, my family would either have to drive thirty hours each way or pay for expensive airplane tickets and hotel rooms.

As my travel was being processed, I waited in the county jail.

I did get to see family before I was shipped away. In a particularly hard visit, my mother said words to me that I will never forget. "Don't ever forget who you are. Don't try to act like them other folks in prison. Don't forget you're a Boggan," she said. "Don't forget your faith. You're smart, so don't act like you're dumb to blend in. You're still my daughter. Nobody or nothing can change that."

My son Bryant asked me, "Mama, when are you coming home?"

I didn't say anything. I swallowed hard, and he dropped his

head. He wouldn't look back up for a long time, because I didn't have a quick answer.

"I'm coming home," I managed to say. "I'm going to fight to come home."

While I was there, I began to call out to God. When I fell to the very bottom, the only place I could look was . . . up. And that's exactly where God wanted me. I remembered that prayer I'd uttered to the Lord when Catina was arrested. I had made a promise to Him, that I'd submit to His will if He would only let her go free. Whatever He had for me, I'd do it.

"Lord, I've messed up so bad," I prayed. "Please show me your will for my life and give me the strength to do it."

Three weeks later, I began my journey away from the family I loved. Officers showed up and shackled my hands and feet. They placed a "belly chain" around my waist, then connected my hands to that chain. My ankles were connected by a longer chain. Then they placed us on a bus.

Traveling while in custody is one of the worst parts of being a prisoner. My leg irons were tight, cold metal cutting into my skin. The temperature in our compartment was not controlled for anyone's comfort, and—no surprise—the windows on the bus didn't open. Every row was filled with sullen, dejected prisoners, packed tightly. The driver of the bus took curves faster than necessary, not taking into consideration the fact that we couldn't stabilize ourselves with our hands and didn't have seat belts. I found it difficult to stay upright. Some of the more experienced convicts pressed their foreheads on the seats in front of them for leverage. Also, they leaned in the direction of the curve when they saw a turn coming up. It took me a while, but I caught on to the tricks that helped a little.

First, we went to the McNairy County jail, in the same Tennessee city where they filmed the 1973 movie *Walking Tall*. I was there for a few weeks before they sent me to a federal detention center in Oklahoma. We drove for hours and hours but didn't go straight. We traveled from one place to the other, so the officers could take breaks, get coffee, and switch drivers. But we stayed on the bus. The convicts couldn't wait to get to prison to get out of the shackles, but I noticed the officers weren't in too much of a hurry. I heard whispers that the guards got hazard pay for transporting us. Time and a half.

Some prisoners refused to leave certain prisons simply so they wouldn't have to be subjected to this sort of travel. The worst part for me was when I needed to use the bathroom. They wouldn't unshackle us, so I laboriously clunked back to the bathroom, where I had to open the door with my handcuffed hands. Once the door came open, I was in this tight, enclosed space. It was very difficult to maneuver pulling my pants down, so I had to ask for help. I fumbled with the door, leaned my head out, and—full of shame—asked a woman seated close to the bathroom to help me. Reluctantly, she came to my aid, though she was handcuffed too and couldn't do it very easily. Looking back, I bet she saw a lot of rear ends that day and resented being seated so close to the bathroom. Though toilet paper was available, the handcuffs attached to the belly chain didn't allow me to properly wipe myself. Some people refused to eat or drink just to avoid such scenes.

Once we got to Oklahoma, we stayed for a few uncomfortable

nights. In the evenings, I noticed women crowded at the windows. One woman was up in the window shimmying, and I had no idea who she was performing for.

"Come over here," a prisoner yelled at me. They were whooping and hollering. My curiosity was piqued. I looked out the window and saw the men's building illuminated from within. In every single window, men were staring at us across the way. Some were exposing themselves, some were dancing, some were touching themselves, some were buck naked.

◇◇◇◇◇◇◇◇◇

One morning, I heard them call me.

"A. Johnson," he barked, before listing the others. "Roll out."

We connected with the Justice Prisoner and Alien Transportation System, nicknamed "Con Air" because it's the highly secured way that convicts travel via airplane. Because federal marshals never wanted us to be able to convey information to outsiders who could potentially help us escape, we were never told of our travel dates or plans in advance. I got up and was strip-searched in preparation for the flight.

"Squat, spread your cheeks, cough," an officer instructed us. And if anyone didn't cough loud enough, she'd say, "Cough again." Guards ran their hands through our hair and looked down our throats. Then we were given another set of flight clothes and were told to sit on a chair that could detect any metal inserted into our body cavities.

Finally, we were shackled, and I climbed up the stairs to the nondescript airplane, which wasn't an easy task with all the chains. I took a look around. These prisoners would be dispersed to their destination prisons in a complicated travel system that prioritized safety above comfort. As I sat on the plane, I felt the cuffs on my ankles again and tried to make sure I had circulation in my legs even though I could barely move.

The women were seated in front, while the men were in the rear. Nothing separated us, but the plane was overwhelmingly male. My travelmates had been convicted of everything from low-level crimes like tax evasion all the way up to rape. We were all treated the same. Desperate hunger darted from some of the men's eyes. Many of the male prisoners licked their lips and made obscene gestures with their faces. I've never seen men contort their faces like that, as they tried to convey sexual desire and emulate sexual activity without the use of their hands. I'd never been more thankful for shackles. It was disturbing to be chained while men looked at me as if I were prey—especially since there were so many of us on the flight and so few guards. I just prayed that we'd survive the trip, and we did. On May 2, nearly two months after sentencing, I arrived at Federal Correctional Institution (FCI), Dublin, in California.

People had warned me so much that I was going to be "with the big girls" now that I was in a federal prison, I'd gotten cowed. But it was less intimidating than I anticipated. This low-security prison was built on the eastern edge of the town and was in an old army post nestled into the mountains. I was expecting a concrete-and-steel prison like you might see on television. Though the walls did have razor wire, FCI Dublin had more green spaces and flowers than I expected. In one particularly pretty patch of pansies was a sign that read NO INMATES ALLOWED BEYOND THIS POINT. The pansies were a bright spot of color in an otherwise drab environment.

I was led into the lobby area to a large desk. When I walked in, conversation stopped. All eyes were on me, as everyone checked out the new arrival. After this pregnant moment, everyone went back to their chattering. This pattern repeated itself with each new prisoner. I later learned this happened for two reasons: each person has the capacity to be real trouble, so everyone made a quick assessment before going back to work. But also, some were checking out the women for possible new girlfriends. The prisoners called new arrivals "fresh meat" or "fresh fish."

A woman came up to me with a welcome pack that included a toothbrush and toothpaste, shower gel, and prison soap. "You'll be needing these," she said in a thick accent. Though I was trying to act normal, she could tell I was out of my element. "Is this your first time?" I nodded, before I was handed prison clothes. I was shuffled from one place to another. Though this was one of the more traumatic days of my life, the officers who were handling me were just doing their jobs. They saw people coming into prison all the time, so they chatted with each other casually, laughing about their life and plans.

I was taken to the "bus stop," where a lot of people were packed into one room with wall-to-wall bunk beds. A&Os—what they called people new to prison, which stood for "admissions and orientations"—didn't get a private space. They broke you in at the bus stop, a holding area so crowded the women could hardly move. I was relieved when they took me away from this area—

because there wasn't enough room. They motioned for me to walk inside my cell.

My final resting place? I had been told I would never leave this prison alive. Two Spanish-speaking ladies were there in my cell. One spoke almost no English, while the other spoke broken English. They were nice enough, even though my arrival meant that three people were going to be living in this tiny cell. It did have a toilet.

Every day, we had to stand to be counted so guards could make sure no one was missing. (They counted us throughout the night, but we didn't have to get up for it.) If a prisoner failed to make it to her cell for the count time, she'd be in trouble. Our cell was so small we couldn't stand side by side. We had to stagger ourselves.

Thankfully, in general population cellblocks, we were allowed to walk outside our cells most of the time. It didn't take me long to get acclimated. After I met my cellmates, I walked around to get the lay of the land. I saw other prisoners in their cells and a prison yard where people could exercise or socialize. I saw a big barn and walked toward it. Inside, I was surprised to see prisoners reading poetry.

I walked in and blended into a crowd listening to a woman at the front holding a piece of paper and emoting as she read. As I was sitting there, I marveled that poetry existed even in a federal prison. A little pop of beauty the officers hadn't extinguished. But I couldn't very well pay attention to the poems. My mind began to wander. I'd never been so far away from my family in my life, and they didn't even know where I was or how far away I had traveled.

I must've looked lost, because a woman in a wheelchair rolled up beside me. "What's your name?" she asked, taking my hand.

"Alice Johnson."

"Alice," she said, as if she enjoyed the way my name rolled off her tongue. Then she looked at me squarely in the face and lowered her voice. "Bloom where you're planted," she said. "God knows where you are."

We stared at each other for a minute. Then she squeezed my hand, releasing me from the trance. As I walked away, I just kept repeating that notion in my mind. "Bloom where you're planted. God knows where you are." Sure, this was a trite saying, a platitude. But, for some reason, her words were exactly what I needed to hear at exactly the right moment. I stopped dragging my feet. Her words gave me a pep in my step.

As I overheard people chatting, I heard them calling each other "Sister" and "Mother." *What a shame that entire families are in prison*, I thought. Then I heard a woman call someone "Dad." When I turned to look, I realized she was speaking to another woman. That's when I realized that women in prison frequently create bonds with other prisoners, because they so crave intimacy. Even if their actual families are not incarcerated, they will create pseudofamilies behind bars to fill that void.

Many called themselves "political prisoners," though I could never tell if their grandiose self-descriptions were accurate. The prison had housed famous criminals. For example, Patty Hearst had been imprisoned there for twenty-one months. The daughter of the newspaper publisher Randolph Hearst, Patty had been kidnapped by the domestic terrorist organization the Symbionese

Liberation Army in 1974. After her father tried to negotiate her release, surveillance videos emerged showing her participating in armed SLA robberies, seemingly of her own accord. While she was at Dublin, her father paid to install balconies on the top floors of the prison's two-story buildings. He also paid for carpet to replace the cold tile in her building, which I was told was the building labeled C/D. President Carter eventually commuted her sentence, and President Clinton later pardoned her.

Also, Stacey Koon and Laurence Powell had been locked up at FCI Dublin. These former LAPD officers were acquitted in state court of violating the rights of Rodney King, whom they and several other officers hit more than fifty times while he was handcuffed on the ground. When Koon and Powell were acquitted, riots broke out across Los Angeles. They were later convicted of violating King's civil rights.

Of course, that all happened before I arrived. However, two prominent people were imprisoned at Dublin while I was there. The first was Heidi Fleiss, known as the "Hollywood Madam" because she ran a prostitution ring that catered to the rich and famous. (Charlie Sheen admitted to paying her $53,000 for prostitutes.) The second was Sara Jane Moore, who was famous for trying to assassinate President Ford in 1975, just three weeks after the Charles Manson devotee "Squeaky" Fromme also tried to kill him.

I never met these two, though I saw them walking around the prison.

To be honest, I was a little intimidated by the fact that this prison had housed so many celebrities. Once, I was chatting with a black woman who told me she was the great-great-granddaughter of Jesse James. The next time I chatted with my family, I told them all about her.

"She's black?" my sister asked.

"Yes," I assured her.

Later, I saw her and she waved at me. I mentioned to someone that my new friend was related to Jesse James. She started laughing.

"No, that's just Edna," she said. "She has mental issues."

I was so embarrassed, and I never told my family that I'd been duped.

I applied for a job working at UNICOR Federal Prison Industries, because they paid more than anyone else in prison, which made it a coveted job. They hired me immediately after I took a typing test. My first role was as an operator who took orders over the phone. Free people called to talk to us about their orders, not realizing they were talking to prisoners. I'd been there only two months when I applied for and earned a job of an Adobe tech illustrator.

One day a supervisor called me into the office to tell me she was so proud of my work. "You are turning out twice the amount of work," she said. "And you just started! Your work is so precise. Normally when someone is just starting, they can do three to five images per day." I took a step back, because I had been turning in ten. "Do you know we sell your images to the government for many multiples of the amount you're paid?"

I was stunned. I was basically slave labor. When I went back to my cell that night, I couldn't stop thinking of how much money I was making for the prison. They paid me no more than $3 per day, but I was making them potentially hundreds per day.

I'm working to keep myself in prison, I thought. *I am making myself too valuable.*

And so I quit and got a job in the vocational department as a vo-tech clerk. I didn't care that it paid almost nothing comparatively. Once my typing prowess became well known, the secretaries for the warden, Constance Reese, would bring me work. Warden Reese was a no-nonsense woman who ran the prison like a well-oiled machine, and she was so kind to me. She'd ask me for my opinion about things, and I received the overflow for all her nonconfidential work. One night I was asleep in my cell when a flashlight turned on right in my face. When I opened my eyes, I saw an officer standing there.

"Are you Alice Johnson?" he said.

"Yes," I managed to say. I sat up, wondering what on earth would necessitate such a visit.

"What's your number?"

"14873076," I responded.

"Okay, get dressed and come with me."

My roommate woke up. "What's wrong?" Sometimes people were taken to solitary confinement, also known as the special housing unit (SHU), in the middle of the night, so it was alarming.

"Come with me," he said.

Apparently, the prison had a volunteer recognition program the following day, which would be a big deal since the director of the Bureau of Prisons was going to be there. However, the company with whom they outsourced the documents had misspelled the director's name and was closed by the time the prison noticed this egregious mistake. The guards led me to the vo-tech room, turned on the light, handed me a big stack of blank certificates, and showed me the error. They gave me a list of all the volunteers who needed their own certificate.

"Can you redo these by the morning?" he asked. "Warden Reese says you are the only person who could possibly help."

I took the huge pile of materials and sat down at the computer. The door locked shut as the guard left. I stayed in there all night by myself, fighting through my sleepiness to get everything done. The prison guard came by and checked on me throughout the night, in addition to the normal counts.

When he opened the doors up the next morning, I stood up, stretched, and handed him a stack of perfectly typed certificates. I'd done it. I had re-created all the documents, and all the certificates were more beautiful than the ones they'd ordered. Warden Reese wrote a nice character letter of commendation to go in my file.

One good thing about working so closely with vo-tech training was that I got to see some of the program's shortcomings. For example, people like me—those with long or life sentences—were not able to take classes for vocational training. The warden gave the short-timers precedence over people with long sentences and those of us who would never see the other side of the bars. Though it made sense in terms of resource management, it caused despair among the long-termers, who had no hope.

How can you tell a person not to hope, not to prepare for her future? People like me should've had some opportunities, right? Being incarcerated doesn't mean that one has to be powerless and remain the same. "Lifer" was just a label, but that wasn't my identity. I decided who I was.

I was Alice.

I had value.

And so did the others who had lifetime and long-term sentences.

I decided to use the respect I'd earned from the warden to ask her to reconsider this policy. I argued it was important for long-term prisoners to work on their outside skills, so they could have a marketable skill once they got back into the world. Eventually she relented, and a certain percentage of people with long sentences could take computer classes. I even convinced prison officials to allow families to come in to see their loved ones graduate as they earned their GEDs. This was the first time they ever allowed visitors at such an occasion—and it was gratifying to see families come and celebrate the successes of their loved ones during visitation.

And it was a good thing that these "lifers" had developed actual skills. Turns out, laws changed. Some of the women with extra-long sentences were released earlier than anticipated, including a woman serving a double life sentence. Because of their new skills, they were able to reintegrate back into society more easily. My friend Cheryl Ward always made sure I got the credit for helping them.

"You got Alice Johnson to thank for this," she'd tell women who otherwise weren't allowed to take classes because of their long sentences.

But I wasn't all about activism and typing. I loved to dance, so I started taking country line dancing classes. I became really good at it, and people would come watch me dance in the barn along with the others. Sometimes while I was dancing and people were clapping, I thought, *Judge Gibbons would be so mad if she saw me having so much fun.* She thought I'd never laugh again.

While I was at Dublin, I sang in the church choir. The prison allowed volunteers from outside the prison to come in and lead a weekend retreat called Kairos, which lasted three days. My group leader was a nun who asked us to close our eyes and imagine where we saw ourselves with God.

"I see these big hands," I told her. "I see myself as a little child, and God is holding me in His hands."

I opened my eyes and was surprised to see she was crying. She couldn't even talk. She reached into her pocket and handed me her card. "This is the order I'm in," she managed to say. The symbol of her order was an image of God's hands holding a little child.

We both knew this was one of those unexplainable God moments.

At the end of the retreat, they gave me a necklace emblazoned with the words CHRIST IS COUNTING ON YOU. I wore it all the time, and frequently ran my fingers along the words to remind myself of this truth. While I was at Dublin, I was at the chapel often. There I watched videos of T. D. Jakes, and his teachings helped me understand the Word even more.

The prison, maybe because it was located in California, had more cultural and artistic activities for us to do than others did. I even wrote a few plays, short productions in which the other women starred. Plus, I sang in the church choir, started a praise dance ministry in church for our services, and mentored women.

While I was at FCI Dublin, I anxiously waited on the appeal that Wayne had filed. In the meantime, I went into the law library so I learn all I could about the law. I had entrusted my life to my attorney, and that didn't work out so well. How did I end up with a life sentence?

I opened those books and learned some very sobering legal realities.

President Nixon had declared a war on drugs in 1971. This new tough-on-crime agenda had unintended consequences and led to harsher sentencing, especially for low-level drug offenders.

When I heard the phrase "drug trafficker," I thought of someone like a member of a cartel smuggling large quantities of illegal drugs across the border. But the federal drug laws established in the 1980s, designed to punish such kingpins, actually now required low-level middlemen to be punished with the same mandatory penalties. These "conspiracy laws" require those only tangentially associated with drugs to be sentenced harshly, and now almost every federal drug crime carries the label "drug trafficking."

I also discovered errors that had occurred in my trial that were not even addressed.

A sense of dread fell over me. I hadn't realized any of this. I'd never heard what a drug conspiracy could possibly entail before going to trial. It was never explained to me what that meant and its possible implications for my sentencing.

In the law library, I met a skinny white lady named Amy Ralston who was always working on her case as well. She had been married to a wealthy man who made the party drug ecstasy. They had been married three years before he admitted his illegal activity to her—and that was only *after* he'd been arrested. While he waited for trial, he asked her to take care of some financial matters that ended up being shady. Because she loved him, she obliged, and she was promptly arrested. Her husband—who'd smuggled millions of pills into the nation—served four years in prison. Amy, convicted of money laundering, was sentenced to twenty-four years with no chance of parole.

Her husband served her divorce papers while she was in prison.

I was beginning to see that sometimes women were affected by the newly defined "conspiracy laws" much more seriously than men.

◇◇◇◇◇◇◇◇◇◇

Even though I was doing my best to adjust to prison life and put my work ethic and experience to good use, mentally adjusting to a life sentence was incredibly hard. Whereas many of the prisoners were counting the days until they would be released, I didn't have that luxury. Other people had a number as a release date. I envied those numbers, because I had only an alphabet.

L-I-F-E.

The worst part about being incarcerated was knowing how hard my imprisonment was on my kids. When we went to court on the day of verdict, I just didn't come back. I had no idea I would receive a life sentence. I know, I know. I had rose-colored glasses, but the duration of the sentence took all of us by surprise.

One day, my kids had a mom. The next day, I was gone. My

daughter Tretessa, who had started her job for Motorola at that time, later said it was a weird sensation, to realize she'd never see me outside prison walls again. In a moment of candor, she said it might have been easier had I died. Catina, who was pregnant, had trouble making ends meet. Eventually, she lost my house and my car because she couldn't keep up the payments. I left her with nothing actually paid for, since I wasn't the big drug lord the prosecutor said I was. Eventually she had to move into an apartment.

It was just as hard for my other kids. My oldest son, Charles, lived on Tennessee State's campus a bit after I left. He dropped out and had nowhere to lay his head. (He did later go back to college, but this was a particularly tough time.) Bryant, who was seventeen when I was convicted, dropped out of high school. (Later, he got his GED and completed two years of college.) Catina offered to let her brothers live with her, but they refused to leave. Basically, Charles and Bryant became vagabonds, sleeping in the attics of their friends' homes and going from house to house. They were living on the streets, and there were times when nobody could find them.

In a moment of frustration, Catina asked Bryant why he wouldn't just move in with her.

"Because this neighborhood was the last place I saw my brother alive," he said. "It was the last place I lived with Mama."

∞∞∞∞∞∞∞

"Did you hear they built high-rises at the Carswell prison?" a woman asked me. "It's the only medical facility for women, and they have to build up the population."

I knew about Carswell. I'll never forget when Judge Gibbons taunted me by rudely suggesting I go there. You know, for my "mental health." Previously, Carswell was just a medical facility with a small work cadre, but now they were asking for volunteers to go there to live in the new high-rises. I was quite happy where I was at FCI Dublin, and I certainly didn't want to go to Carswell.

I put it out of my mind. When I first got to prison, I had no idea that transfers were even possible. I went to FCI Dublin believing it would be my final resting place. I had made my peace with that reality.

A few weeks later, I saw the warden in the dining room.

"I saw your papers come across my desk." She smiled. "I recommended that you get transferred to Texas."

"What?" I asked. "Why?"

"I know you want to be closer to your family," she said, acting as if she had done me a favor.

It was true that my family hadn't been able to make the trip all the way out to California. I'd had two visits: First, Julius came. Then Thelma and my nephew Chad had come. Of course, I missed them so much. However, this new correctional facility was still over five hundred miles from Memphis. Though it would get me closer, it would still be prohibitively expensive for my family to visit. It wasn't a day-trip, that's for sure.

I could tell the warden was happy to do something for me, but I really didn't want it. Regardless, because of her, I got bumped ahead of other women who had volunteered to go to the new prison.

After only one year at FCI Dublin, I was gone.

Chapter 8

When I arrived at Federal Medical Center, Carswell, in July 1998, I had to swallow my disappointment. I saw big buildings, razor wire, steel, and concrete floors. Since this was the only medical center for prisoners with special medical and mental health needs, it was filled with sick women. As I looked around, I saw women in wheelchairs, prisoners on crutches, and highly medicated people with dazed looks on their faces.

I was dismayed. I'd gotten comfortable in my California prison, made friends, and created a space there for myself in which I was valuable. Needed, even. Suddenly I was lonely and uncomfortable, and my family still wasn't able to come visit me all the way in Texas. That night, I climbed into my bed, closed my eyes, and began to pray. I sought the Lord more than ever during that first month at Carswell.

Bloom where you're planted. God knows where you are.

If it was true at Dublin, I told myself, it had to be true at Carswell.

I began reading the Bible even more earnestly while I was at this new prison. Sometimes I'd follow a "read the Bible in a year" pattern; other times, I'd pick a topic after a word or phrase would hit me. I would go to the library and dig into the references. I might study one aspect of God for months. I had the time. Slowly, my sadness over leaving FCI Dublin lifted.

"You don't act like a person with a life sentence," everyone from staff to prisoners said to me after I adjusted to the new prison. "I had no idea," they would say. I even had one person tell me, "Something must be wrong with you. How can you be happy sitting on a life sentence? What kind of medication do you take?"

"I don't take medication," I said, realizing they were detecting the joy of the Lord in me—not mere happiness. "What do I take? I take in the Word of God, and I eat it."

And feed me He did. My typical day at Carswell began at five thirty. We had to wait until count was completed before leaving our rooms, so I'd take some time in prayer and was out of my cell around six o'clock. I'd head to the showers, where there would be long lines of women waiting for their turn. That took some getting used to. In California, the showers were scattered around— there might be two stalls here and two there. But in Texas, the showers were situated all together, and there was always a long line.

Breakfasts at the chow hall included all-bran cereal, grits, fruit, and oatmeal. I usually ate something, then headed to work until lunch break. I always worked, using the twelve-cents-per-hour salary to help pay for long-distance calls. For lunch, they served a slice of pizza or an artificial chicken patty. In my mind,

I could imagine my mama looking at that chicken and saying, "Slop."

Although the food wouldn't have met my mother's exacting standards, it was fine. Unfortunately, I developed an allergy to Red Dye 40 and peanuts. That meant some days I actually couldn't eat what they served, so I'd have to make something in my unit. My family kindly made sure I had enough money to buy snacks from the commissary. There, for a little more money than the real-world cost, I could buy rice, tortillas, coffee, ramen soups, cookies, crackers, pudding, ice cream, chips, canned meat, cheese, condiments, and other items. Plus, the prison allowed us to take any one piece of fruit (apples, oranges, bananas) with us to eat later in our cell. Some people managed to sneak other food out—potatoes, cheese, sugar, butter, you name it—but I had no idea where they hid it on their body. (I didn't want to know!) With their smuggled ingredients, they were able to make dishes we couldn't make with our commissary items.

I met a new friend named Chanel Jones, and she always enjoyed eating my concoctions. We got all our food the legal way, and I was able to make pretty good meals using what we had available. I could even make a decent birthday cake, if I could buy Hershey bars and cookies. Though we had a microwave for our unit, we sometimes had to wait hours for it. Alternatively, we filled thermoses full of hot water, put food in a baggie, and dropped it into the hot water to cook. Some people used the iron to melt their cheese, but that was a bit too far for me.

In the evening, some watched television in the atrium, which had a couple of screens in a special room. The first one to get the television would determine the programming, and I was never interested in their selections. Sometimes something racy would come on the screen in the evenings and people would yell out, "Don't look, Miss Alice!" I guess I had the reputation of not being entertained by smutty things. "You don't need to see this," they'd say. Or they might clarify, "You don't want to see this."

I didn't need the warnings, because the television never really held much allure. With a lifetime sentence, I found that it wasn't terribly important to know what was going on in the outside world. If I really wanted to watch television, I'd get up early and tune the television to the inspirational shows on TBN or Daystar.

Instead of watching television in the evenings, I'd hang out with Chanel, keep a journal, or read novels in the evenings before lights-out. Also, I'd attend rehearsals—whether it was dance, drama, or a project I might be doing for one of the departments. At night, we had a ten o'clock count, so the lights went out around ten thirty.

◇◇◇◇◇◇◇◇◇◇

Chanel and I used to walk around the exercise track every day. We counted our laps around the quarter-mile track to make sure we got enough exercise to stay in shape. As we walked, we chatted. What's weird about prison is that eventually you learn just about everything about a person in there. In the outside world, people's lives keep developing like a play unfolding with more news and drama. But inside the walls of a prison, life sort of stalls. Chanel told me her secrets and I told her mine. Then all we had left to chat about were the things happening in the prison: drama at work, which guards were crooked, and who was fighting with whom.

All the normal cliques existed at Carswell, except everyone was female.

The wealthier prisoners walked around flaunting their new belongings—food, contraband, tennis shoes—while poorer ones went through the trash to snag any discarded items. Drug users figured out a way to be high as a kite, while others avoided the temptation of drugs in prison. Pushers sold drugs somehow right under the guards' noses. There were also skinheads, Black Panthers, white supremacists, witches, pagans, and rednecks. There were troublemakers who went in and out of the SHU as if it had a revolving door. Others were Christians, like me, whom people liked to tease over our perceived virtue. (Once, some people criticized the fact that Chanel and I didn't allow sexy dancing on the praise team—it should go without saying that dancing unto the Lord should not look like you are dancing in a nightclub—and they told Chanel they were going to "baptize her in her own blood." Without saying a word, I put on my boots, went down, and paid them a visit. I wanted them to know that I had Chanel's back and that she was not alone. "Don't play," I told them. They immediately backpedaled.)

Some people wanted to talk endlessly about what their lives used to be like before prison, while others always talked about what they were going to do, eat, and buy once they got out. Some wanted to retry their case to you. Others never would tell what crime they'd committed. Just like on the outside of prison, people tended to hang with their own type of person.

In general, I tried to bring the same interest in helping people that I'd had at Dublin to my new life at Carswell. Since Carswell was a hospital prison, the wheelchair brigade formed a large portion of the population. Many had special needs, so I worked on creating Special Olympics–type events just for them. We were the only prison that ever did anything like that, and I received special recognition for my involvement and leadership.

Also, since so many people were sick, I trained to become certified as a hospice worker to help these women die with love. It was not an easy certification to get, because I had to learn how to do basic care for the infirm—like how to turn the sick over in bed, brush their teeth, change their linens, and help them go to the bathroom—as well as learn about the psychological and spiritual dynamics that help people die with dignity, how to treat them with proper bedside etiquette, and how to deal with grief. To die alone, in a lonely place, takes away the last bit of dignity a person has. Prisons are not meant to be nursing homes, so they can't satisfy all the needs of a dying prisoner. And since many of such prisoners were abandoned by family members long ago, many die alone. I shuddered every time I thought about it.

After my training process, I graduated and began the hard work of helping people die well. Every day, I grappled with the cold reality that one day—since I had a life sentence—someone might eventually help me die in prison as well.

"Here's your next assignment," the prison nurse said, handing me a clipboard. "She's comatose, she's dying, she's deaf, and we need everyone to take a shift."

I went to her room to sit with her and saw the woman in bed.

Her mouth was open, her eyes were open. That stare of hers un-
nerved me, but I didn't look away from her. Whenever I sat with a
hospice patient, I first liked to find out from her friends what her
religion was or some things that she liked.

When I asked around about my people, I made sure I didn't let
curiosity get the better of me and ask why they ended up in prison.
This was especially true in my hospice care, because I didn't want
to feel different about anyone. The sad fact was that some of my
patients were probably child molesters. In prison, they called these
sex abusers "chomos," a derogatory nickname that derived from
the term "child molester." These women were treated so badly,
because their crimes were some of the most horrific crimes imag-
inable.

I tried not to go there. Who knew the circumstances that led
people to a life of crime? Maybe they were on drugs. Maybe they
had been abandoned. I didn't know. But I did know that if people
were locked up, they were paying for whatever they did. God can
handle administering justice better than the women at Carswell
could. I let Him handle it, but I wanted to treat everyone with
respect.

As I asked around about this new patient, I discovered she was
Catholic. Since I had worked in the chapel as a clerk, I set up for
every Catholic service for the chaplain, Father Vincent Inametti.
That meant I was pretty familiar with some of the songs they
sang. For my patient, I read to her from a Catholic book as well as
the Bible. I flipped through the pages and landed on Psalms, since
I didn't know what her favorite scripture was. Perhaps it didn't
matter, since she couldn't hear the words. But as I was reading, I

remembered a Spanish song I used to hear the Catholic prisoners singing called "Ten Piedad." This translates to "Have mercy."

I closed the Bible and started singing, "Oh-oh Lord, have mercy, oh Lord, have mercy, oh-oh Lord, have mercy, have mercy on me."

By the time I got to the end, I noticed a single tear had rolled from her eyes. Amazed, I stopped for just a second. Were my eyes deceiving me? Could she hear me? Did she actually understand what was going on? I opened my mouth and started singing the song more.

"Oh-oh Lord, have mercy, oh Lord, have mercy, oh-oh Lord, have mercy, have mercy on me."

Tears by this point began running from her eyes. I got up and went to her bed. Her face was exactly the same—the same vacant stare and her mouth gaping open. But now her face was wet.

I was almost afraid to speak. Had this woman been trapped inside her body in a prison as she died and had no way to communicate?

"If you understand me," I said hesitantly, "can you blink your eyes one time?"

I stepped back, my heart pounding in my chest.

She blinked.

"Would you like to see your family?" I asked. "If so, blink twice."

Now, I don't know why I asked that lady if she wanted to see her family. We were in prison, after all. Her family had stopped coming long ago because they couldn't bear to come all that way to see her and then not be recognized. However, I knew that when a person got to a certain stage of near death, the warden would allow family members to visit even in the prisoner's room.

She blinked twice and my heart felt like it stopped. Once I collected myself, I ran out and found the nurse. "She can hear."

"No she can't, Miss Johnson."

"I asked her a question and told her to blink. She was able to do it," I hurriedly explained. "Please come and look."

The nurse ran and got the doctor to test my theory. Sure enough, this woman had been mentally present the entire time. The prison contacted the family, who came up immediately to spend time with her and communicate using the blinking method. It wasn't much, but it was so much more than she'd had. She was no longer alone.

After her family left, she died within the week.

◇◇◇◇◇◇◇◇◇◇

As I did in Dublin, I threw myself into the work of the church. While I was in Texas, I was introduced to a prison ministry called the Potter's House. I started going to their Bible studies and working for the chapel. I was selected as the person who did the welcome and announcements (much like my mother always did). Also, I started working with the dance ministry there. I became the lead choreographer and dance team leader. I acted as a mentor to the other prisoners, teaching them how to serve in the various roles. When we would go into the chapel to rehearse or perform various tasks, I'd take a group of ladies with me to show them the ropes.

During the time I was at Carswell, we had a succession of

three head chaplains: Bill Berry was first, followed by Joseph Pryor, and then Robert Danage. Each had more than his share of work to do in prison. Sometimes prisoners would line up outside their offices, waiting to speak to them about their problems or prayer requests. Sometimes I'd go out to the people in line to offer a listening ear. "Is there anything I can do to help?" I'd ask. Many times, people would tell me what was going on in their lives, and I would pray for them right then and there. Then they'd get out of the line and go on with their lives. This became so common that the chaplains would frequently tell people to "go see Miss Johnson" when they were busy with other duties.

I loved listening to and empowering women. I didn't desire to have any official title in the church, a preposterous idea anyway. People in prison could not become ordained as official ministers. The only "title" I needed was one of servant. I wanted to serve the women in a way that could help them see goodness, even in prison.

Some days, this was harder than others. Especially on holidays. Mother's Day, Valentine's Day, and Christmas caused the women to reflect on how they'd celebrated those days when they were free, the unbidden memories causing pangs of regret. But I didn't want that sort of sorrow to take hold of these women. I began a "holiday ministry" of sorts. I would put on uplifting holiday-related programs and decorate the chapel to make them feel like they weren't in prison at all. It was just one of the things I did to keep people's spirits up.

One evening, I had a dream. In it, I saw a pulpit that was empty.

"Why don't you go get behind it?" my friend in my dream asked.

I didn't go, so she urged me again. Reluctantly, I walked to the pulpit and stood behind it. The next instant, I saw people flocking to it, as if they were there to hear what I had to say.

Then the scene changed. I was with a seven-foot-tall man wearing a white robe. In my dream, I believed him to be an angel.

"Do not be afraid," he said as he touched me on the shoulder. "Everything you have ever done in life has prepared you for this."

<hr>

Powerful as it was, that dream felt like just that: a dream—that is, until I was visited by another messenger, this one in person. Outside ministers would come in frequently to evangelize in the prison, and the women were always excited about one in particular: Dr. Linda Holliday. Not only was she a powerful woman of God who sometimes had prophetic words, her husband, Kene, was an actor who starred as Detective Tyler on *Matlock*. That celebrity piqued the interest of the prisoners, and her chapel services were full.

In September 1999, I was a part of the choir as she delivered a sermon. She described herself as a prophetess, so I slunk down in my seat trying not to draw attention to myself. There's no telling what might come out of her mouth. I imagined if she stopped to give me a message from God, she would reveal some of my past sins. I didn't necessarily want everyone to hear about all that right there in the chapel.

When she wrapped up her sermon and was about to leave, she

closed her eyes. It was almost as if she were meditating. Then she began walking down the aisle. As she got closer to me, I thought, *Don't let her stop.*

She didn't know me from a cat, and I was pleased when she passed me. But just as relief came over me, she jerked. It was almost as if a puppet master had pulled her backward. She took a few steps back and stopped beside me.

"You!" she said.

I looked up at her.

"Have you ever been in ministry on the outside?"

"No," I said, sheepishly.

"The Lord is calling you into the ministry, not by the will of man but the will of God."

The whole chapel was quiet, watching this unfold. Prisoners do not become ordained in federal prison. It's just not done. Ordination requires having witnesses to your spiritual walk, which are hard to come by when you are behind bars. Plus, prisons are not eager to have imprisoned women take roles of responsibility and leadership. Prisoners are supposed to be prisoners, and that's that.

In normal circumstances, I wouldn't have believed this woman, but images of the pulpit dream I'd had the week before rushed through my mind. I began to stand up, because it felt like the right thing to do in the moment.

"No," she said, stopping me. "Let me bow before you." Then she got down on her knees and prayed that I would be a woman of faith who would walk out my vocation. It was a moment I'll never forget, the moment I received my calling from God. It happened to be on September 5, the day I got married to Charles so long ago. In my life, no one had ever asked me to spend my life with them—Charles never proposed, since our marriage was arranged by our parents. However, on this day, I was invited to take a journey with God. And I answered "Yes" with my whole heart.

My relationship with Linda did not end there. I began writing letters to her and writing essays for her ministry's publications.

For the next few years, I continued to do the work of the Lord, fight for my freedom and the freedom of others, and mentor and counsel women. Since Carswell was a medical facility, I saw a lot of physically infirm women, but perhaps even more commonly, I saw broken women who were in need of spiritual healing. When many of them confided in me and shared their pain, I noticed it often included a burden of unforgiveness.

With sudden clarity, I realized I had not fully moved on myself. I had to go through my mind and list the people who had hurt me. I had to release myself from the bitterness. I had wrongly believed I had the right to be angry and unforgiving toward the people who had caused me so much pain. Bitterness was causing my soul to rot. Through unforgiveness, I was giving my past and others power over me. I could no longer live with the stench of my own anger and had to do what seemed impossible: forgive them.

By making the choice to forgive, I took away the power of unforgiveness and took back my life. What freedom I experienced when I did! People have asked over the years how I was able to stay so positive about life in prison, and forgiveness is a big part of my answer. Being able to forgive gave me back my life.

This newfound freedom gave me an opportunity to share my testimony with others.

"Let it go, Stacey," I told one young woman. "It has nothing to do with them, but everything to do with you."

Stacey snapped her fingers. "Just like that! I'm supposed to act like it never happened? That they never gave me up and lied on me to save their own skins? My own sister—my blood—my friend, and her sorry, no-count husband? I can't! I hope they both burn! I ain't no saint, Miss Alice. This is real talk."

I encountered many other Staceys over the years, and I felt like I could speak into their hearts. At one time in my life I *was* a Stacey, but I had chosen to forgive everyone in my trial, including myself. My pain was not wasted, because it birthed a message of life-changing forgiveness I delivered repeatedly to other women over the years.

Though I loved ministering, there were no real routes available for prisoners to become ordained. Plus, I wasn't seeking to become a minister of the gospel. We're all called to minister the gospel; I didn't need official papers to designate me as such. And so, I was just doing what I do—helping others and attempting to serve the best way I knew.

Four years later, on October 23, 2003, a group of Christians gathered in Panama City Beach, Florida, at a conference called "God's Millennium Women: A Time of Refreshing." For years, I contributed to the materials that Linda used for these outside women's conferences that included sermons, poetry, and prayers. The pastors related to this ministry—Apostle Prezell Lane, Apostle Dr. Linda Holliday, Evangelist Kene Holliday, Minister Vicki Jackson, Minister Vickie Webb, and others—became familiar with my work and compared me to what the Apostle Paul did: proclaiming the gospel from behind prison bars.

I could accept this comparison only because, like him, I too was a chief among sinners. I was in prison proclaiming the gospel to people in the outside world, but the Word of God knows no bounds or restraint.

I wrote a sermon called "Master, Can You Still Use Me?" about the biblical account of Jesus making a special trip to reach out to the woman at the well, a person whom society had shunned because of her lifestyle. I saw myself in that woman. The message came to me when I was on my knees in prayer. I remained on my knees as I wrote the sermon.

When Linda's husband read it, he decided to minister it to the women himself. A newspaper article reported that these women were so emotionally moved by this message that they called out in repentance, "Master, can you still use me?" It became almost a mantra. These women were physically free, but they felt the need to be spiritually free.

The people who regularly attended these conferences were very familiar with the woman who wrote from behind prison bars. They bore witness to the effect of my ministry to the out-side public. Chaplain Pryor provided witness to my ministry on the inside of prison.

Pastor Lane and Dr. Holliday and Evangelist Holliday per-formed an ordination service for me by proxy. Though I had not sought this title, I became an ordained minister of the gospel of Jesus Christ. This is one of the greatest honors of my life.

On November 6, I went to the chapel. Linda was coming back to speak and had requested that I do a worship dance prior to her talk. I created a dance to the song "Alabaster Box," a song inspired by the woman described as a "sinner" and someone who "had been forgiven much" in the gospel of Luke. In all likelihood, she was a prostitute who came to Jesus and treasured the ointment in her alabaster box, a symbol of her great devotion to Jesus and her great need of him. If I was honest, I could admit that I had more in common with the prostitute than the Savior. Of course, this is true of everyone, but it's easier to see the reality of your sin when it's landed you in prison.

I danced to that song and then sat down, settling in for what I assumed would be another normal service. But then Linda came forward with a packet of papers in her hand, and her whole ministry team came and stood behind her. She took out a bottle of oil and called me up. Unbeknownst to me, Chaplain Pryor had allowed them to come in and have an actual ordination ceremony for me. I was shocked. This was not allowed under the rules, since prisoners were not allowed to be perceived as emerging leaders.

But that was exactly what happened. Chaplain Pryor later told me that he recognized the call of God on my life, and that he had to obey God, not some arbitrary prison regulations.

⬦⬦⬦⬦⬦⬦⬦⬦

Despite all the work I was doing within the walls of Carswell, I was still trying hard to achieve my freedom. The appeal process was a great deal of work, but it afforded me the opportunity to have another set of eyes look at my case. I received my first denial of appeal on October 4, 1999, and many more would come. I filed appeals and motions as much as possible, because I wouldn't even be a candidate for clemency until I had exhausted all my appeals. Once, when I got an email notifying me of the status of my appeal, I noticed that the appellate judge had been copied on the denial. Judge Gibbons, the same judge who presided over my original trial, had now been appointed to the United States Court of Appeals for the Sixth Circuit. I worried about whether this would make the process more difficult for me, and I hoped the judge would recuse herself from any decisions on my appeals.

In 2004, I was working to file a motion pro se, because my attorney Wayne Emmons had long ago abandoned me—and he'd done it in person. Five years prior, I was shocked at the news Wayne delivered to me in prison during what I thought was a routine attorney's visit. My direct appeal had been recently denied, and I assumed he was visiting so we could talk about the next step. Instead, he started with an apology.

"I just wanted you to know that I'm sorry how things worked out," he said. "But I have grandchildren that I want to see grow up. I need to think about them."

I didn't understand what he was getting at. It felt like he was sort of apologizing to me for having to take care of himself and his family instead of me and mine. That should not have been a conflict, since my family had paid him over $50,000.

"Whatever you have to say about me, just say it," he said. "Whatever you have to do, just do it." He paused, then looked me straight in the eye. "But I cannot and will not help you anymore."

I stood up, looked at him, and said, "You're pitiful." Then I walked to the officer guarding the visitation room and said, "I'm ready to go."

I never looked back. I would have to fight for myself.

The next year, the Supreme Court made a landmark decision in *United States v. Booker*, which eased some of the harsh consequences of drug-related offenses. It made the sentencing guidelines advisory rather than mandatory, giving judges much-needed leeway. Also, it disallowed *estimated* drug quantities, so a prosecution had to present the actual weight of drugs seized instead of the "ghost dope" that had been offered up as "evidence" in my case. Regrettably, none of this ruling was retroactive. If my sentencing would've occurred after this ruling, I wouldn't have been sentenced to a life in prison.

∞∞∞∞∞∞∞

I put my hand on my mouth.

"You've been doing that all week," my cellmate Kenya said. "What's wrong?" I'd started having pain near a couple of my bottom teeth. With all I had been through dentalwise, tooth pain was something I took seriously.

"You need to go get that checked out," Kenya urged. Since Carswell was a medical facility, I figured I'd go to the prison dentist and everything would be okay. I walked into the dental facility and described the accident that had caused me to have to get dental implants. Then I showed them the teeth that were giving me trouble.

The dentist took an X-ray and looked in my mouth. "Your implants need to be scaled." Implants sometimes need scaling, which means they have deposits on them that need to be scraped off with certain instruments. "We don't do that here," he said. "How long are you going to be in prison?"

"I have a life sentence," I said. "But I don't believe I'll do all of my sentence."

A wave of disbelief washed over his face, and then he continued. "You're going to have bone loss, because you'll get food trapped around the implants. And we don't have the proper instruments for the maintenance of implants."

And that was that. In prison, you can't get a second opinion; you can't look online for alternatives. Since my prison didn't have the tools to take care of dental implants, they couldn't take care of them. Or wouldn't.

"We're going to have to take them out," he said.

Take them out.

I'd had my teeth taken out before, when I had that wreck and they were jolted out of place by the impact of the accident. After years of work, effort, and saving, I had been able to get these teeth replaced. And now they were telling me they were going to take them back out of my head, for the lack of a relatively inexpensive tool.

But I was in pain. I was a prisoner.

Absent any other options, I agreed to what seemed like a barbaric solution. This was no simple procedure. They shut down the dental department and brought in dental students to watch what they might never see under normal circumstances. They gave me anesthesia through an IV, and I slipped out of consciousness. When I awakened, my mouth was numb and I felt out of it. They put me in a wheelchair, and one of the dental assistants pressed a prescription into my hand.

"Go to the pill line to be administered Percocet," she said. "Three times a day."

When the anesthesia wore completely off, I got a mirror out and opened my mouth. My teeth were gone, and I stifled a sob. Then, when I looked more closely, I noticed that my gold tooth— the little secret thing I loved about myself—was also gone.

The next day, I went back for a checkup, and I demanded, "Where's my gold tooth? That was not an implant, that was a crown."

They looked at each other, then said, flatly, "We must've pulled it out on accident."

I couldn't believe my ears. "Where's the gold?" I asked. Something about the injustice of it all struck me so hard. These people had taken a part of my body out accidentally and somehow misplaced the metal. It reminded me of articles I'd read about how Nazi soldiers were instructed to sort through the corpses of Jews they'd killed in the gas chambers. Using dental pliers, they'd first have to pry open the mouths of the victims, sometimes frozen shut because of rigor mortis. Then they'd look through their mouths and pry out the teeth that had gold in them.

I don't want to be melodramatic. I was not murdered by Nazis, I was not the victim of a genocide; I had pain medicine and was in a sterile environment. But these are the thoughts that went through my mind when my tongue felt the hole where my secret gold tooth had been . . . and I slowly realized they'd yanked out something that I loved about myself.

Chapter 9

❦

When women arrive at prison, they are frequently broken, guilty, and full of shame, victims in need of the message of forgiveness. So many are in need of healing from the Great Physician. I know I was.

The church plays a very important role in the life of prisoners. It is seen as a place of refuge, a place that fills spiritual needs, a place where you can safely come and try to find a better path than the one that led to incarceration.

We all felt the loss when Chaplain Pryor received a huge promotion and had to leave. However, we were also blessed when his replacement, Robert Danage, became the new supervisor and head chaplain of the religious services.

Chaplain Pryor tried to ease him into his role by explaining the ins and outs of all our activities. "You have to find Alice Johnson," he told him. "She'll be able to help with anything."

Chaplain Danage did seek me out—which wasn't hard, since I always ended up at the chapel no matter what other jobs I landed.

After I told him some of the details about the activities that we did there, he asked me if I had ideas about how to improve them. Of course I did. And we began to make the spiritual lives of the women even better—regardless of their race, culture, ethnicity, social status, or faith orientation. We provided religious programs and activities for all recognized faith groups: Protestant and Catholic, Jewish (Reform and Conservative), Muslim, Buddhist, Hindu, Wiccan, Jehovah's Witness, Seventh Day Adventist, Mormon, Rastafarian, Native American, and many others. If anyone had a problem, regardless of her religious beliefs, I made sure Chaplain Danage was aware of her crisis.

There were also several other chaplains who worked in religious services. One of them was Father Vincent Inametti. He was a charismatic Nigerian Catholic priest who loved to sing and had an infectious smile. But I started noticing some inappropriate contact with women, and I no longer felt comfortable working at the chapel. I found another job.

Any officer in a prison has an inordinate amount of power over the prisoners, and it is illegal for them to use that power for sexual favors. Plus, Father Vincent was supposed to be married to the church, not seeking romantic fulfillment among his charges. I knew a woman named Mercedes who'd told us that she had been a prostitute before prison. One day, she revealed that Father Vincent had been turned on when she confessed details of her former life.

She was laughing about the fact that her confession had caused a physical reaction in the priest. That was her goal. I couldn't believe my ears.

A couple of days later, I was headed to my regular dance rehearsal when I passed Father Vincent's office and noticed his new clerk was cooking food for him in the chapel microwave and serving it to him.

When I stepped back, waiting to get music, I noticed her giving him a very familiar look. Their eyes seemed to linger on each other too long, before she came out and handed me the music. I gave her a disappointed look, but she returned my gaze. It was as if she was bragging that she'd caught his attention and had allowed me to see their attraction. She wanted me to witness it.

When he hired another clerk, more rumors started flying: he had two women working at the chapel. Jealousy erupted among all these women, and I could no longer ignore the gossip that Father Vincent was a predator. I wish I had gone to the prison authorities, but they are trained to believe that all prisoners are liars. And the only proof I had was what seemed to me to be a meaningful glance. However, even though I was just a prisoner, I felt a spiritual obligation as a believer to confront him.

"Father Vincent, what you are doing is wrong," I said to him after going to his office.

He acted confused but didn't speak.

"You are compromising yourself and the women." Anger flashed through his eyes, but I wasn't going to stop. I leaned forward. "I know what you are doing. You don't know how far you have fallen, and you need to stop it."

"Who are you to chastise me?" he said as he stood up. "You can leave."

And so I did.

A few months later, rumors were flying around that Father Vincent was in a lot of trouble. I was told that Mercedes had gone to the chapel and pulled back a heavy blue curtain. Normally this curtain covered the chapel's sound system and other worship tools. But on that day, she pulled back the curtain and Father Vincent's true nature was laid bare. He was committing a lewd act with a prisoner, and he didn't even pause when he got caught. Mercedes contacted the Office of Inspector General.

A short time later, I was told to report to the chapel. When I arrived, I saw boxes outside Father Vincent's office. When I stepped inside, I noticed tears in his eyes.

"Have a seat," he said. Gone was the anger and self-righteousness I'd seen before. "You were right. I should've listened to you."

I just looked at him for a moment, and he continued. "I want to apologize to you. I'll be leaving soon, and I hope you do well."

Before me, I saw a broken man. I silently got up and left.

That same day, I saw guards walking him out the front door. Only after I was free, after an internet search for his name, did I discover that the warning signals I'd perceived around Father Vincent were spot on.

In 2008 he pleaded guilty to multiple charges of sexual abuse of a ward and was—ironically—sentenced to federal prison for forty-eight months. The sentencing judge called his actions "surprisingly heinous and shocking."

In 2010, two women sued the Catholic Diocese of Fort Worth and Bishop Kevin Vann, claiming Father Vincent had abused them and other women in other parishes and the diocese ignored this information. They further alleged the diocese still allowed him to become a chaplain in an all-women prison, which was like letting the fox guard the henhouse. The two victims settled for an undisclosed sum.

Now that I've learned the rest of the story, I am deeply saddened that already vulnerable women were put in harm's way. I never knew what caused most people to end up in prison, but many women have a history of sexual abuse and deserve to be protected while there.

◇◇◇◇◇◇◇◇◇◇

One friend I had at Carswell was Sharanda Jones. We gravitated toward each other because we were both first-time, nonviolent offenders who had life sentences. (Though she had the same last name as Chanel, they were not related.) We both loved to laugh. She had been at the prison for a while before we got close.

Sharanda had been a cosmetologist before she was arrested and worked as an instructor at Carswell's cosmetology school, where she taught the prisoners to cut real hair after a certification process. (They ultimately could take the state cosmetology board exam and become licensed.) We could receive free haircuts, braiding, highlights, color, twists, conditioning, but—since we couldn't take products back to our cells—the hairstylists had to pick up our products from the commissary before our appointments. Plus, we could get only one thing done at a time. If a woman got twists, she couldn't also get a deep conditioning. Appointments were spaced out every three weeks.

The salon seemed like any other cosmetology school you might find on the outside and was well equipped with brand-new, clean equipment. It had chairs in the waiting area and a radio playing music. The prisoner-beauticians put a cape over your clothes and a towel around your neck just as if you were a free woman. If you closed your eyes, you could just imagine for one moment that you were out in the world getting your hair done.

In addition to working in this prison salon, Sharanda did the hair of women in the maximum unit (since they weren't allowed to go to the prison salon) and in the hospital unit (where the women were too sick to get their hair done in the prison salon). This allowed her to see her mother, Ms. Stribling.

Yes, her mother was in prison too. With all the thousands of drug convictions and sentences involving family members, it was common to see multiple generations of the same family incarcerated at the same prison.

When Sharanda was only three years old, her mother had a terrible automobile accident that left her a paraplegic. They had very little money, and Sharanda had to fill more of a parental role for her siblings. To get money, Sharanda became a middle-woman between a cocaine buyer and a supplier. Like me and like Amy back at FCI Dublin, she was accused of being involved in a drug conspiracy, even though she was neither the supplier nor the buyer. Sharanda's criminal conviction was her first, felony or otherwise, but the prosecutor "enhanced" her charges with extraneous accusations. At the end of the day, the judge had no choice but to sentence her to life in prison. Her mother was also arrested and was serving her term at Carswell. They were both beloved and a big part of our church community.

When Sharanda's mom died, the prison alerted me before they

told her. They knew this would be a major blow to Sharanda, so they thought it might be a good idea for me to provide a shoulder she could cry on. But when I went down and told Sharanda, I cried more than she did. I absolutely loved her mother and I couldn't stop crying. I was no good.

"I can help with the memorial service," I offered between sobs. I was frequently asked to participate in the religious services and events—memorial services, baptisms, release celebrations, and so forth. I developed friendships and mentoring relationships with so many of the women that I played an important role in providing support and assistance to them in the big moments of life and death. Sharanda accepted my offer to help her with the service.

Chaplain Danage frequently held memorial services for prisoners who passed away. Many prisoners and even the prison staff members attended these services, but the prison allowed a volunteer ministry team from the outside to come in for Sharanda's mother's memorial.

I sang, conducted a praise dance, and, along with a select few women, spoke in Sharanda's mom's honor. It was so beautifully done and absolutely packed, it seemed like it was an outside memorial service. So many people knew and loved Ms. Stribling, and it was a beautiful way to commemorate a life that held so much pain.

⬦⬦⬦⬦⬦⬦

Over the course of my prison time, I was in charge of preparing rooms for various religions' worship times. Once, overcome with curiosity, I asked the Jewish worshippers if I could come hear the shofar being blown for Rosh Hashanah. I enjoyed hearing the instrument that King David had used in the temple orchestra and the instrument used to declare war.

"Oh, Miss Alice," my friend lamented. "We don't have anyone to blow it this year." Apparently the rabbi had another commitment, and the Jewish women who attempted to blow the shofar could not produce the sound.

"I played the French horn in high school," I said. "Want me to give it a try?"

They did. A few days later, the rabbi presented me with a shofar and tried to find out if I knew how to make it sing. It came naturally to me. When I blew it, the sound pierced the air. The unique, bellowing sound definitely got everyone's attention. The rabbi had tears in his eyes and the women too.

Everyone came to a complete standstill.

"I thought the end of the world had come," one of my prisoner friends told me later. It was a wonderful moment for me, because I knew my Jewish friends could not have properly worshipped without it.

I thought it was important for everyone to be able to exercise their faith. One day, I heard that the Buddhists were being treated poorly, so I doubled up on my efforts to be kind to them. I went through extra-special efforts to prepare for their worship time, which came around every Friday.

"Alice, you treat us so nice," one of the Buddhists named Laurel said. She worked in the education department teaching computer skills. "I heard that Christians are supposed to be all about love, and I can tell that you are a real Christian."

Her comment meant a great deal to me. I served all the faith groups in any way they needed me. It was my job. It was my honor.

◇◇◇◇◇◇◇◇◇◇

In 2004, my friend Mrs. Hatcher, who was bound to a wheelchair, rubbed her hands together nervously. "I just wanted to see that movie so bad."

"What movie?" I asked.

"*The Passion of the Christ*," she said. "Mel Gibson's movie."

"We can watch it eventually," I said, but she shook her head.

"No," she said, weakly. "It's rated R."

R-rated movies were not allowed in prison, and there was no exception for religiously themed films. Many of the ladies were crying because they couldn't see it, especially since so many people were talking about it on television.

"Well, when you get home you have to see it," I said, trying to be encouraging to Mrs. Hatcher. There was never any guarantee that anyone ever would be "home." She was really distraught, so I went back to my room and sat on my bed. In my sadness, I felt like I received a message. I didn't hear it, but I felt it in my bones: *You write it.*

"Me?" I asked as I prayed. "Write a passion play?"

You write it.

I went to Chaplain Danage and told him about this idea. "I want to do a play," I said. "For Easter." He knew I did quick skits to help illustrate his sermons, with very little preparation. I'd also done several shorter works before, such as one about Ruth, another about the woman caught in adultery. The skits were just ten minutes, but I'd never done a full-length play of this scope.

"I think it'd be great," he said. I knew he had no idea I was going to comprehensively cover this topic. But I meant to go big. There's really no other way to cover the greatest event in all of human history. Whereas Mel Gibson's movie was *The Passion of the Christ*, I named my play *The Life and Passion of Jesus Christ*. I planned on my play being even more epic.

At the time, I had four Bibles. I opened one up to the book of Matthew, one to Mark, one to Luke, and one to John. I dug into each of these four books, representing the gospel literature, for every piece of information the Bible offered about Jesus's life and death. I developed characters, including Malchus, the servant of the Jewish high priest, whom I'd never seen developed as a character. I even wrote all kinds of minor characters into the play to bring them to life and give the women more speaking parts.

One day, Laurel came by and saw me pecking away on a typewriter. Just as she passed, she saw me rip the page from the typewriter in frustration. I'd made a mistake and had to start all over. Though fine for forms, typewriters were less than ideal for a play. "I wish I had a computer so I could save this, and not start over every time I want to add or change something."

"What are you doing, Miss Alice?" Laurel asked.

"I'm trying to write a play for Easter," I told her, believing that as a Buddhist, she wouldn't understand why this was so important to me. She turned and left without saying a word. Little did I know that she went straight to her boss.

A few minutes later, Laurel came back to me and said, "I'm going to type your play for you on the computer." She had told her boss that I was trying to do something good for the church and asked if she could type my new "Jesus play."

"She said yes," Laurel gushed.

Something about how she didn't even ask my permission, she just offered up her services to me, was very touching. Very needed. It was only four weeks before Easter, and I had just started. That meant I still needed to write the play, make costumes, and cast the roles.

"Thank you so much," I said, handing her one solitary page. I also dug into the trash and gave her the papers I'd thrown away. She looked back as if to say, *This is all you have?* Her help allowed me to do all the other necessary tasks to get this play done. As I was writing the play, my hands were moving so fast it felt like they were on fire. I felt like my creative juices were really flowing, when Laurel showed up with a perfectly typed first page. "Here you go," she said, handing me the page. "Do you have more?"

She was fast, which meant I could go even faster.

I gave every spare second to this play, even though I had gotten a higher-paying job in the commissary. This caused me to push rehearsals into the afternoon, write late at night, practice with people during my lunch break, and continue to cast the characters.

Chanel had just cut her hair into a short style. "You're going to be Pontius Pilate," I told her.

"Is it because of my hair?" she protested. No one wanted to portray the guy who oversaw the crucifixion of Jesus, but I needed to cast someone in that role. "Because I look like a boy?"

She was sick of all the drama associated with her haircut, but I didn't have time to be tactful. "That's exactly why," I said, laughing. "You look like the perfect man." I had to duck to dodge her fist.

Casting was difficult, because everyone expected a certain amount of holiness in these biblical characters like Mary the mother of Christ, the angels, and Jesus. However, I decided not to choose the most Christian people to fill these roles, but instead selected people who didn't know anything about the Bible. I chose people with behavior issues, which meant they'd stay out of trouble so they could attend rehearsals and wouldn't end up in the SHU. I picked people who weren't familiar with the gospel story, so they wouldn't rely on their old Sunday school lessons for inspiration but would encounter the material anew. For the role of Jesus, I picked someone no one expected. I loved giving prisoners the chance to do something they didn't realize they could do, to stretch their imaginations and consider living in this amazing story.

I put out a call for artists, for people who could make props, for seamstresses, for anyone who had a willingness to put her hands to this work, and people came from everywhere, excited to help. Josette's sister Tracey answered the call. Even though she was in a wheelchair, she made herself available to do whatever was needed. From making props to ironing costumes, she was so happy to contribute. It was wonderful to be needed, and she took great pride in her work. One completely bald woman who was four feet, eleven inches tall named Nae showed up. On her scalp, she had a tattoo that read F——YOU. Though everyone was shocked at her arrival—she was in and out of the SHU all the time—I took one look at her and put her to work. She painted the sets, decorated the big auditorium, created art, and worked day and night. When I was struggling to figure out how to create a tomb for the set, she came up with a clever, realistic design that we could set up and take down quickly. She became my right-hand woman and was a more faithful worker than I've ever seen. People were always shocked when they saw her working, because she was known for her cynicism.

It may have looked and felt disjointed, but I found order in chaos. I learned multitasking from my mother, who, as a chef, had an amazing ability to balance many duties and had a keen sense of timing. Since I wrote the entire play, I knew all the parts backward and forward and worked with every single actor.

"This is how I want it done," I said one afternoon during a rehearsal. I jumped up on the stage and enunciated the lines. "You've got to feel this person. Don't give me a monotone. This is a real person. Embody your person."

I acted out the scene the way I envisioned it, then looked back at the prisoner-turned-actress. "Now you do it." When I jumped off the stage, a young black woman with straight long hair was standing there. She stretched out her arm.

"Hello, I'm Brittany Barnett."

"Nice to meet you," I said, giving her about half of my attention as I watched my actress onstage attempt to tweak her performance. I was in fast motion, and her introduction had slowed me down.

"I'm a law student," she said.

"Uh-huh," I said, taking a break from our conversation to bark some orders. "More feeling," I said to the actress onstage. I looked back at the young law student. "Nice to meet you, but I must get back to my work."

As I was walking away, I heard someone whisper to Brittany, "That's Miss Alice. She's the female Tyler Perry around here." I laughed. I *had* written a play called *Madea Goes to Carswell*, which was pretty hilarious. And I'd done a presentation for women who were arriving at the correctional facility for the first time called "Prison for Dummies." But this was a bit more epic, and I didn't have time for small talk.

During the rehearsals, we worked hard. And then, during the days, I dreamed about the play as I worked in other areas. Frequently I'd be working at the commissary and see Laurel knocking on the back door.

"I want to know what happens next," she said. "Do you have more pages for me to type?" Since she was a Buddhist, she didn't know how the story turned out. I smiled when I thought about how she'd receive the surprise ending. As I worked in the commissary, I kept a Bible right there on the counter and outlined possible dialogue. Sometimes I'd break out laughing at the scenes in my head that were unfolding as I rushed through the store and filled orders for people. I'd jot down some of the scenes on paper bags, if I ever forgot my paper. No telling what my customers thought about me at the time. But as soon as I'd finish a page, I'd slip it under the door to Laurel.

It came together just in time. Two days before the show, Laurel handed me the last page. "Miss Alice, do you think I could come to the show?"

"Only if you sit in the front row," I said. "I reserved the best eight seats in the house for you and your friends." To my utter surprise, people started coming in and didn't stop. We had to do four performances. The first night made accommodations for people in wheelchairs. It seemed that everyone in the compound, which housed 1,800 people, attended over the course of the performances.

As people milled into the room and saw the decorations, I loved seeing the delight on their faces. I don't think people expected such a big event. We had seventy speaking parts and one hundred crew members total. The entire play was two hours long.

I had a role, of course, which involved dancing. Right before I went out, I noticed that my toes didn't look very good, and I was to perform barefoot.

Sharanda looked down. "Yeah, we need to do something about that."

Of course, you simply can't maintain any sort of beauty regimen in prison, and we didn't have access to pedicures. Improvising, Sharanda got out glue and glitter, "painting" my toenails in the only way we knew how. We knew it wouldn't stay, but we figured we'd do what we could.

The performances were powerful, and all our hard work had paid off. When I went out to dance, I danced with all my might. The glitter, of course, began to come off. But the light caught it in such a way that the audience was mesmerized. There I was, performing in a cloud of sparkling light. They assumed it was an intentional effect, instead of simply a temporary, inadequate solution. In prison, I'd learn time and time again that you can really survive and thrive just by utilizing what you have.

Over the course of the show, people felt many different emotions. They laughed at certain scenes and cried at others. I incorporated meditation during the play, to give people time to reflect, and I could tell that the audience really enjoyed themselves.

At the end of the show, the play received a standing ovation. Many people were in tears over what they had seen and what we—together—had done.

I was still amazed by what we'd accomplished when, after the performance, I ran into Sharanda.

"So you met Brittany?" she asked me.

I looked at her blankly.

"Barnett?" she continued. "The law student who is trying to help me get outta here? She said she met you during rehearsal. You were standing on a table or something."

I laughed. I didn't realize it at the time, but I had met one of the women who would play a role in my release.

Chapter 10

My family means so much to me, so I desperately wanted to connect with them as much as possible while I was in prison. That meant I lived for phone calls.

For 23 cents per minute, I could talk to my family members. Pretty steep for someone who made twelve cents per hour. The prison justified the cost, saying it had to pay people to monitor the conversations. They had to make sure we weren't doing anything wrong on the calls, like having a three-way call or planning something illegal. Every few seconds, the call was interrupted by a recording.

This call is from a federal inmate.

For almost $70 per month, we received 300 minutes, which I tried to spread over 20 calls 15 minutes in length. This was tough, since I always found it impossible to tell my family member I had to go.

One day, I called Tretessa, and I could tell from her voice that she was crying. When I heard her distress, my stomach immediately churned.

"What's wrong?" I asked. She told me that my son Bryant was in trouble. Still anchorless from my imprisonment, he fell in with the wrong crowd and was arrested for computer fraud. He'd gotten into minor trouble before, but this was not minor.

"Please talk to him, Mama," Tretessa begged. She knew the dangers of going to trial, the way that people will come out of the woodwork to testify against you—people you have never met—to get a better deal for themselves. "If he's convicted, he might get thirty years in prison."

Bryant was good hearted, very handsome, and tough as nails. Still, I didn't even want to imagine what life in prison would be like for him. My heart was broken. I felt so powerless, sitting in a federal correctional institute in Texas, trying to communicate with my son in his county jail via the postal service. But that was my only option.

I begged for him not to go to trial, after what had happened to me. I asked him to just settle and get what he could out of the system, to pay the price. They offered him three years, but he refused.

"I can't afford three years in prison," he wrote, telling me he opted to go to trial. My heart sank as I read those words. I felt like I was reliving my own past failures. I felt responsible, since I hadn't been there to guide him as a mother. He ended up being sentenced to nine years, and eventually he ended up at Kingman prison in Golden Valley, Arizona—one of the worst prisons in America. And so, I became a pen pal to my son, prison to prison.

I had tried so hard to give my kids a better life. I remember holding Bryant's little chubby hand in the welfare line, wondering what sort of example I was showing him. In spite of all my trying, however, he ended up in jail. Just like his mama. The pain of this was hard to even process.

It helped to receive his letters, though I wasn't always happy to hear what was going on over there. They called him "Memphis." I shuddered to think about my son in such a place.

I held out hope that somehow we both would be free. Even though my attorney Wayne had told me he'd stopped filing motions, I believed that the truth would come out. Though I had committed a crime, I had received a penalty that far outweighed my offense. But in 2010, I received news that one of the people who knew the truth was dying.

My sister Coria told me over the phone that Wayne Emmons was in terrible shape. She knew this because she and her husband, Samuel, had been involved in Memphis law enforcement for over thirty years each and had both retired as majors. Because they knew Wayne, they had followed his life after he had been my attorney.

At seventy-two, Wayne had long ago stopped practicing law. He was one of those southern lawyers whose reputation, attitude, and personality supersedes their actual career. He practiced law for only fifteen years before going on to become a comedian. Wayne also consulted with John Grisham—who had grown up right there in Southaven—on some of his characters. This relationship earned him small roles in movies. He told people that he was tired of dealing in "human misery"—which I can confirm is exactly what his legal career had wrought.

"Samuel and I are going to go to the nursing home to visit him," Coria told me. She hoped that maybe his conscience had been pricked and that he would finally tell us the truth about whatever was going on with my case that caused him to fail to represent me wholeheartedly. We always thought he'd done a bad job, and his subsequent visit at Carswell created even more questions. Was there more than just incompetence at play? He'd acted afraid and fearful, almost as if someone had pressured him into downplaying my defense. My sister hoped that going to his bedside would give him the opportunity to come clean.

She told me that the visit began well. They were kind to him, and he returned their kindness as they reminisced about old times. But when Coria brought up my name, his eyes narrowed and his previously lucid conversation turned into babbling.

"It seemed suspicious," she said. "Like he didn't want us there."

I pressed the phone against my ear. I probably shouldn't have had any expectations about the visit, yet I did. "Then what happened?" I asked.

"He ended up calling security," she said. "He said, 'Get them out of this room!'"

Of course they left. They didn't want to upset a man in a nursing home. He later died, and with him, any hope of getting real answers about his role in the case that landed me behind bars for the rest of my life.

This call is from a federal inmate, the automated system said.

But we didn't need the reminder.

In 2013, I received a letter that gave me much-needed hope. It was from a woman named Jennifer Turner who worked at the

American Civil Liberties Union (ACLU). Jennifer was an attorney who was searching all over America for prisoners like me, whom she dubbed "the living dead." Someone had given her my name, and I took a moment to read the letter even though *The Life and Passion of Jesus Christ*—my epic play—was just about to go into its tenth annual production.

"Dear Ms. Johnson," her letter began. "I'm contacting you because I'm doing a report on prisoners charged with nonviolent crimes who had been sentenced to life in prison with no chance of parole."

Well, she got the right person.

In her envelope, she included a profile form. She'd also included her email address and asked me to add her to my Corr-Links account, which gave her the ability to email me directly. I was honored that she'd reached out to me, and I tucked her letter away in my cell so I could come back to it once I had the time.

I'd received the letter two weeks before Easter, so I couldn't stop to fill it out. My first Easter play was such a huge success that I'd put it on every year. The crowds never got smaller, and news of the play went through the Federal Bureau of Prisons, which everyone called the BOP. Whenever women transferred from other places, they always wanted to know about this play they'd heard so much about. News travels, even throughout the prison system.

My friend Sharanda asked me if I'd sent back the forms to Jennifer.

"Not yet," I said, as I continued to work on a prop for the play. She began to chastise me, since she had already sent her forms back to Jennifer. In addition to this report, the ACLU was going to launch an ad campaign to draw attention to the fact that there were so many nonviolent prisoners serving life sentences. Sharanda began to preach to me, something about how faith without works is dead, but I interrupted her.

"Now hold it right there," I said. "I'm going about my Father's business, and I know He'll take care of me."

Finally, once the play had run its course, I sat down, filled out the forms, and added Jennifer's email address to my access list. A few days later, I received a message from Jennifer acknowledging receipt of my forms, which she described as excellent. We began corresponding and she got to know Tretessa, whom she interviewed for the project. They became close, and Jennifer was impressed by the fact that my family had never stopped fighting to bring me home.

When I heard that a new prison was being built in Aliceville, Alabama, I realized that I could at least get closer to home. My heart raced when I realized this prison would be only three hours away from my family. Though they had been faithful to keep in contact with me, it had been hard to physically see them while I was in prison.

In May 2000, my sister Thelma had it laid on her heart to take my mother and father on a road trip. My mother had been so excited that she'd get to see her baby. I didn't realize it, but Mama always referred to me as "baby," even though I wasn't the youngest child. "I wonder how my baby is doing?" she'd say. Or, "I'm so proud of my baby." I always kept in touch with letters, phone calls, and homemade cards—I never bought my mama a card. I decorated them with hearts and included photocopies of photographs I had in my cell to make them special. I spent most of my money on phone calls to her and also sent her these physical reminders so she'd have something to read and hold when she missed me. I was in closer contact with her than even my own children, because I wanted to keep her uplifted with the good things I was doing in prison.

My sister had stretched out the ten-hour drive so my parents could rest along the way. They finally arrived one summer morning, bright and early as soon as visitation opened. Though it had been only four years since I'd last seen her, Mama looked remarkably different. When I left, she had been a strong, robust woman. She was much thinner now. We had "contact visits," meaning we were in the same room. We were allowed only a quick hug before the guards would tell the prisoner to separate from her guests. But when I saw Mama, who was wiping away tears, I ran to her. We embraced. I don't know how long, but the guards looked away.

"You look so good," she said quietly in my ear.

Once we settled down, I sat as close to her as I could. Daddy bought candy out of the vending machine, which we ate together. (I must've inherited my sweet tooth from him.) The tears quickly turned into laughter as I relayed funny anecdotes about prison life. I told them about how I'd been filing motions by myself, and I promised to make them my homemade chocolate cake when I got out.

"You're going to live with us when you get freed," my mama said. "We still have your room ready." I agreed to this unlikely scenario, silently.

While we chatted, the guards came over and told my parents nice things about me. The duty officer that day was the head of the psychology department. She told them of the work that I had been doing to help the various departments put on their programs. It was an encouraging time, and the faces of my parents were beaming when they heard these guards bragging on me.

They were the last ones to leave at three o'clock when the visitation ended. When my daddy began to pray, we all began to cry. "You hold your head up, now," my mama said before she left. It was the last time I'd ever see them together alive.

Now as I contemplated leaving Carswell, I recalled that memory as well as so many others I was leaving behind—both happy and sad. Carswell was the place I was living when my father died in 2007, it was where I created the Easter play, and it's where I developed another prison family.

Still, those memories couldn't compete with family. When I found out that I could possibly be closer to my family in Alabama, I signed up for the transfer. I could be closer to my kids this way, and the chance of more frequent visits with all of them was too good to pass up. But when the approval list came out, my name wasn't on it.

"What's going on?" I asked my counselor.

"You have too many medical restrictions," she said casually. Apparently, because of a previous knee injury, which made stair climbing more difficult, I had an asterisk by my name. Since that knee had long since healed, I felt this was suspicious reasoning. Turns out, they simply didn't want me to leave since I had gotten so involved in prison life at Carswell. Was it possible that I'd integrated myself so thoroughly into the life in prison that they weren't ready to lose me?

Thankfully, after I protested and pleaded my case, I got approval to go.

On the last Sunday before I left, I went to chapel.

Chaplain Danage was happy that I'd gotten the transfer, but he was sad to see me leave. "Alice in Aliceville. There's a nice ring to that," he said. "Alice is going to Aliceville for her destiny."

He called me up to the front of the chapel and laid hands on me.

"Give her mercy," he prayed. Then the Holy Spirit came over him, and he made a prophetic utterance. He was careful not to disrespect the rule of law and also careful not to give people who had life in prison false hope. But suddenly, his usual caution and conservative language vanished. Instead he spoke it out that I would be able to go home before I died. People in the church all witnessed this prophesy.

It was a hopeful moment. Did the fact that he made such a strong statement indicate that it was truly a message from God? I firmly believed so. But Deuteronomy has a fail-safe way of telling whether a person is a true or a false prophet: "When a prophet speaks in the name of the Lord, if the word does not come to pass or come true, that is a word that the Lord has not spoken."

In other words, time would tell. Regardless, a sense of awe fell in the chapel, and we all rejoiced. Then, after fifteen years of my life behind those Texas bars, I was on the next bus out.

Chapter 11

It was August 15, Catina's birthday.

I got out of the transit van and stretched my legs, feeling every mile of the trip to Federal Correctional Institution, Aliceville. The shackles had prevented me from even standing up straight, and I had certainly aged since the last time I'd had to endure the indignities of prison travel. The ankle cuffs had cut so badly into my legs, my ankles were swollen and I couldn't walk right for a couple of days. Plus, being in a moving vehicle had taken some getting used to after all that time.

I took a look around.

Gray concrete. Steel. Drab. No flowers. The people in Aliceville were so happy to have this new prison, which was a project of then-Alabama senator Jeff Sessions. This prison was a higher-level security, because it had been initially built for men. When we first got there, we had to pass through metal detectors just to walk in our unit—which meant I had to take on and off my steel-toed boots. (They later changed this policy.) We had big steel doors that shut and they locked us in at night beginning at nine thirty. Though at Carswell we were allowed to come out later in the evening, we couldn't leave our cells at Aliceville. Each cell had a toilet and a distress button to push if you had an emergency. I hated being locked in for the night, and I began to feel like the walls were closing in.

I didn't care. This was just another place to sleep, a place much closer to the home I left, to the family I loved.

Aliceville was a tough place to visit. Visiting someone in prison is not the most pleasant experience for family members. Unaccustomed to prison life, mine had to emotionally prepare themselves for seeing me locked up. After driving three hours, my family then had to go through a metal detector. Though prison rules prohibited them bringing in their purses or bags, they could bring twenty dollars' worth of coins in a clear plastic bag to use in the vending machines. Plus, the dress code regulations weren't obvious. Of course, visitors couldn't wear any immodest clothing, anything that showed too much skin in the front or the back. But they also couldn't wear white or khaki clothing, slippers, open-toed shoes, spandex, leggings, underwire bras, and other items. The rules were so onerous that the prison suggested visitors bring an entirely different set of clothes just in case.

Once, my nephew JT had to go buy new clothes because he'd worn khakis, and he had to go to Fred's to pick up some acceptable clothing. Our visits had to be concluded by three o'clock, and the people who visited had to be on my approved list. They had to fill out a form, and they had to receive written approval well in advance. I had a huge family, so I wanted everyone to come at once. Though this had been permitted at Carswell, Aliceville had more severe restrictions that allowed for only five visitors at a time unless there was advance approval.

I'd been there only one week before my family showed up.

∞∞∞∞∞∞∞

On September 23, a little over a month after my arrival, my mama died.

When I was first locked up, she'd called Tretessa crying all the time. I think Mama cried more than I did about my being in prison, and that just broke my heart. At the end of our phone calls, she often asked me, "Are you coming home for Christmas this year?" She'd pose this question even in January. Her hopefulness shook me to the core.

"I'm fighting to get there," I would say, shocked at the question, swallowing back the tears. "Mama, I'll never stop fighting to get back to you," I always said.

But while I was at Carswell, our conversations had grown dimmer, and I didn't hear the hopefulness in her voice as much, as the early stages of Alzheimer's were setting in. The disease had begun taking its toll on my mother, and I ached over the realization that she might diminish and die without me by her side. But that's exactly what happened.

I was so sad that I couldn't even go to her funeral, but I participated in her service by writing a piece called "Mama's Legacy."

"My mama, Sallie Mae Boggan, was a great woman of God and my hero. She left a legacy that you won't read about in a history book." I went on to write about her faith, courage, integrity, love, and sacrifice. At the end, I wrote, "Mama, I thank you for the legacy that you left us. May we never forget it. And may we all strive to represent and honor your great name with the way we live our lives." It pained me to have to write this from behind the walls of a prison. Not only because I missed being able to attend my mother's funeral and mourn her properly, but also because I knew that my incarceration was so deeply troubling to her. I regretted causing her one second of pain.

Even though I'd known for a while that Mama's death was imminent, it still grieved me.

I wrote Jennifer and told her that my mother had died. And she emailed back with a bright spot of good news. "You have been selected as one of six prisoners—four men and two women—to be featured in the ACLU ad campaign that will be in major news publications."

Is this the media associated with my release? I thought, recalling all those dreams that people had told me over all these years.

My selection for the ad campaign lifted my spirits, and I couldn't wait to tell people the news. For so long I had fought for my freedom, but no one had even seemed to notice. None of my motions had gone anywhere. My faith had been tried over and over and over. Some people doubted I'd ever be free, and others doubted even my sanity.

A prisoner named Jacquie, who used to be at Carswell, overheard people chatting about the new ad campaign while they were working in the kitchen. "Don't believe her. She's been talking for years that she's getting ready for the cameras. She's crazy," Jacquie said, her voice dripping with cruelty. "She hasn't seen a camera yet."

But my belief never wavered.

When the ad was published on November 3, it was everywhere. Julius was standing in line at a convenience store when he picked up a *Jet* magazine and saw an article on the gymnast Simone Biles, who would be an Olympian. On the other page, he saw my face looking back at him. He had no idea that I'd even given an interview, so he was a little shocked. But it appeared everywhere—in the *Washington Post, The Nation,* and in almost every major publication.

When the magazines arrived at prison and people began seeing the ad, people ran up to me excitedly. When I encountered Jacquie—without her knowing I was aware of her doubt—she said, "Hey, hey, hey . . . There's the celebrity."

Jennifer's report, released in conjunction with the ad, was a powerful reminder of how many people were in the same boat as I was. "These are the stories of scores of prisoners who have been warehoused and forgotten, locked up for the rest of their lives for nonviolent drug and property crimes," she wrote. Of course, I was just one of 110 case studies. And we were just 110 case studies of thousands of Americans who were being warehoused. Most of the life-without-parole sentences in the report were the result of laws requiring mandatory sentences, laws targeted at habitual offenders, statutory penalty enhancements, and other sentencing mandates. When the ACLU investigated the cases, they discovered that in many instances the sentencing judge believed these mandatory sentences were too severe but couldn't do anything but obey the laws.

I was pleased to see Sharanda's face featured in her report as well, though I hadn't been able to keep in touch with her much since I left Carswell.

I hoped that President Obama would read my story and grant me clemency.

∞∞∞∞∞∞∞∞

I was in the third group of prisoners who arrived at Aliceville's prison, so it wasn't well established as a prison yet. We had a chaplain, but he wasn't Protestant. To fill that void, the Pickens Baptist Association provided ministers for us. Working with them, I started ministry programs inside the prison, introduced plays, created activities, and came up with the name of the church: Aliceville Body of Believers. Later, they called me a "church planter" for my work there. Also, I blew the shofar once again for Jewish prisoners, because there was not a regular rabbi there. Plus, I helped the Muslims utilize some of the more Christian programs, which empowered prisoners with tools for reentry into society. Since the wonderful Christian people of Aliceville hadn't had much experience dealing with other faith groups, they appreciated my ability to accommodate all the various faiths.

Aliceville was closer to family, but there were trade-offs when it came to security.

In April 2014, the prison put all of us with life sentences on a two-hour watch. From six in the morning until they locked us in at night, I had to report to an officer every 120 minutes. Supposedly, this was to prevent someone from breaking out of prison. Or, if someone did break out, they'd at least know about it more quickly. Typically, the at-risk prisoners were put on watch, those who were escape risks, leaders, disruptive, or high profile. However, since we "lifers" had nothing to lose, they figured we might just try anything to get out.

Believe me. We weren't getting out. Aliceville was surrounded by razor wire that would cut a prisoner into ribbons if she ever got tangled up in it. I'd been in prison eighteen years by this time, and I had tried to escape precisely zero times and had clear conduct. How on earth did they think I was going to leave? Weirdly, the women who had actually tried to escape weren't even on the watch. It felt ridiculous to be targeted like this after so many years behind bars.

In prison, it is possible, though not easy, to forget that you are caged like a trapped animal. For example, when the radio at the salon happens to play your favorite song. Or when casting the perfect person for a role. If, just for a moment, I could imagine being anywhere else, the prison brought me back to reality every 120 minutes as I scurried to find a guard. If I awakened at six o'clock, then I had to make sure I checked in with someone at eight, then at ten, and so forth. They even made you check in during visitation from family members, even if you were being watched over by a guard. My life was increasingly punctuated by indignity.

And the consequences of forgetting were serious. One afternoon, I checked in with the guard and went to chapel, one of the few places the sound of the intercom didn't reach. I was preparing for worship, humming a song to myself, when my friends burst through the doors, their faces stricken with panic.

"Miss Alice, what are you doing?" they asked, out of breath. "They're calling! Please check in!" I ran out to find the busy guard I'd checked in with as I heard my name being angrily called out over the prison system. They were about to shut the entire prison down and do a recall for count.

"Alice Johnson, you must report to a guard immediately."

The guard sheepishly admitted he had forgotten to pass my info along to his higher-ups, but because of my friends, I was able to clear it up before I got put in isolation. Another time, however, I was so busy working on a project I actually forgot, and it was my fault. I was engrossed in reading at the library when I glanced at my watch, which read 5:58. My heart sank. I ran out of the library to try to find a guard, but didn't see one until 6:05.

"Will you call me in?" I asked nervously. But just then, I heard my name over the intercom.

"Alice Johnson." They'd already begun writing me up, but ultimately that ended with only a reprimand.

I wrote up a grievance about this unnecessary practice, and I encouraged others to do the same. Finally, they relented to our requests and gradually retired this system. It was a happy day when the prison guards posted a list of the women who no longer had to check in. My friends and I ran to the list, and my eyes scanned down the names. Some of the people listed were known trouble-makers. On the first run down the list, I didn't see my name. So I started at the top. Slowly, with sorrow, I realized my name wasn't actually there. Some of the women around me burst into cheers, others burst into tears.

"Are you still on the watch, Miss Alice?" someone asked me.

"I wonder why Alice is still on the list," others said beneath their breath. "I thought she'd be one of the first ones to come off." Gossip was one of the main activities in prison, and me being on the list felt like a statement about my worth. Though it was disheartening, I was glad I didn't come off with the first group. Some of my good friends were still on the list, and this allowed us to share in our common suffering.

I was on the two-hour check-in until the next list came out. That meant five months of two-hour reminders that my time was not my own.

◇◇◇◇◇◇◇◇◇◇

On April 23, 2014, a surge of excited chatter flowed through the prison. Most of the prisoners were in correspondence with different advocacy groups who sent out regular emails that made us feel that we weren't forgotten. But on that day, the prisoners received emails explaining that President Obama—midway into his final term—had announced a new clemency initiative encouraging qualified federal prisoners to petition for reduced sentences.

When I started the clemency process, I had already filed at least eight unsuccessful appeals. In 2011, I had received my first clemency denial, but I still wouldn't give up. Since you can't re-apply for clemency immediately, I had to wait for a full year to apply again. On December 31, 2013, I had received my second denial letter. This seemed like a chance to change all that—a real reason for hope.

People were invigorated by the news. The harsh War on Drugs laws that began in the 1980s had landed many behind bars without hope for release except clemency. It had always seemed very unlikely that the president of the United States would take notice of criminals wasting away in correctional facilities—until now. I eagerly jumped in line to get access to a computer, and when I got there I discovered that the president had spelled out six precise criteria for possible clemency. The prisoners had to:

1. be serving a federal sentence in prison, and, by operation of law, likely would have received a substantially lower sentence if convicted of the same offense today;
2. be nonviolent, low-level offenders without significant ties to large-scale criminal organizations, gangs or cartels;
3. have served at least ten years of their prison sentence;
4. have no significant criminal history;
5. have demonstrated good conduct in prison; and
6. have no history of violence prior to or during their current term of imprisonment.

As I read every one of these criteria, my heart surged with joy. Not only did I meet all of them, I exceeded them. I had 100 percent clear conduct for my entire time in prison with no disciplinary infractions. I was a true first-time nonviolent offender. I probably wouldn't have received such an extreme sentence had I been charged years later. I'd served eight more years over the minimum ten years' requirement spelled out in the criteria.

Since I'd been in prison, I'd worked in the prison's chapel, business office, food service administration, and hospital. I'd trained to be a hospice volunteer to help dying prisoners, coordinated the Special Olympics–type events, mentored other ladies through the Choosing Healthy Alternatives and New Growth Experiences program, helped prisoners get their GEDs, taken and excelled at educational and vocational training programs (like Spanish-language classes, clerical and computer skills courses, and self-help programs), and written and directed many plays. Not only did I lead the prison's praise dance ministry, I even became ordained as a minister. And I'd done all this to help empower myself and other women, even though I had been given zero chance of ever walking out of prison again.

Still, I'd need help if I was going to file for clemency. I sent out multiple letters to attorneys and asked if they would agree to represent me pro bono now that the Clemency Project 2014 had been announced. The first to respond was Marcia Shein, an attorney who was a national expert in sentencing, appeals, and postconviction relief. With her generous help, I was ready to go.

Attorney General Eric Holder estimated the president would make ten thousand clemency grants. Surely, with my record, I thought, I would make that cut. I prepared my materials, including a letter from my warden about my accomplishments. They wrote about all the work I had done and how I'd helped make prison life more bearable for others. My family and friends had gotten personal letters from congressmen Bennie Thompson, Steve Cohen, and Mark Veasey. Family members, members of the clergy, celebrities, the local Mississippi chapter president of the NAACP, and even the former chief of police in Los Angeles wrote letters on my behalf. (Now that my story had gone national with the ACLU ad, many people wanted me to go free.)

My packet was huge, and it included a progress report that described me as an "exemplary prisoner." I had so much support, I began mentally preparing for my life outside prison. I dropped my materials into the mailbox, and my application became one of thousands that poured in from across the nation. So many petitions flooded the White House during the Clemency Project 2014 that President Obama gained the distinction of receiving far more requests than any previous president.

Many such appeals involved crimes like murder, sex crimes, terrorism, public corruption, and financial fraud. The Justice Department waded through all of them, weeding out the applications that fit the criteria to make sure that they landed on the president's desk during his administration. I wasn't worried. Because I met or exceeded all the criteria, I had faith that I would definitely make the cut.

In July 2015, my friends at Aliceville were sitting watching the television, their eyes glued to the screen. "Miss Alice, he's getting ready to do it," they said excitedly. "President Obama is about to announce more clemencies."

But I had other things to do besides wait on another list. I had just graduated from a program called "Rubies for Life" that taught prisoners how to reintegrate into society. The graduation was happening that day, and I had a role in the ceremony. I danced to a song called "The Battle Is the Lord's." One of my friends, Alice Latula, stayed behind to watch the television so she could bring the news to me at the chapel. The atmosphere was electric, because we were certain that I was about to be granted my long-awaited clemency.

I danced, then settled into the graduation ceremony. But my eyes kept scanning the crowd for my friend who was supposed to bring me the good news. She was nowhere to be seen. That's when I realized. Though President Obama had released forty-three people, I hadn't made the list. When I came back from the graduation to go to my cell, people could hardly look me in the eye.

After that, the clemency lists began to come out more frequently. In December 2015, President Obama announced another ninety-five commutations. Everyone hurried to the computer room to see if they had made the list. I quickly saw that my name was not included again, and my heart sank. But people told me that Sharanda, who was still in Carswell, was on the list. Though I was sad for myself, I rejoiced for her. I knew she'd be a blessing to the community outside these bars. I was also happy that her lawyer Brittany Barnett had championed her cause. Sharanda and I couldn't talk, so Brittany passed on a message. Sharanda told me, "I'm heartbroken that you weren't on that list. I know you were just as deserving."

Back home, my family worried that I might be upset over my omission from so many clemency lists, so Coria, Julius, and my niece Ashley decided to take a road trip to cheer me up.

"Okay, everyone, we need to take a pilgrimage to Aliceville," Julius told them. "No doubt Marie is devastated, and we can't let this get her depressed." When they walked into visitation, they had a steely-eyed determination to help me overcome my despair. When they arrived, the guard came to get me out of my cell, and I danced out of it.

"Miss Johnson," he said. "Are you the happiest person here?"

"This is not happiness," I corrected him. "The joy of the Lord is my strength."

When my family saw me, they threw their heads back and just laughed.

Julius exchanged glances with the others. "You do realize you were not on Obama's list, right, Marie? Or did I miss something?"

I grabbed his hand and danced with him. They just so happened to visit on children's day at the prison, and people were pouring in to see their mothers, aunts, and grandmothers who were locked inside. A prisoner was acting as deejay, music was blaring, I was line dancing with Ashley, and they were serving pizza. We had a blast.

Coria sang "Best Thing That Ever Happened to Me," by Gladys Knight.

"Oh, there have been times when times were hard," she sang. "But always somehow I made it, I made it through." I closed my eyes and remembered those days when I heard her singing, back when we were picking cotton and her spirituals lifted my soul.

The hours flew by, and it was one of the most memorable days I had in prison. As they left, I called out to them. "Be strong," I said. "Don't lose hope."

They turned back and just laughed. "We drove all the way down here to tell you that," said Julius.

∞∞∞∞∞∞∞∞

"Get to your rooms," we heard over the loudspeaker. It was February 2016, and the commanding voice made almost two thousand women at Aliceville take notice. We were used to announcements like this, if someone pulled the fire alarm or if a fight had broken out. *Another lockdown*, I thought, hoping it wouldn't affect dinner. But there was a panicked quality to the announcements. They were rushing us. "Drop everything. Get to your rooms now!"

When we got into our cells, the doors locked behind us. My cellmate Karina climbed onto her top bunk and I sat on the bottom, awaiting further instruction. It was too early in the evening for us to have eaten yet.

Something was seriously wrong.

"What's that?" I asked Karina. It was getting dark and still. Suddenly I heard a loud, ominous whistling sound coming through the thick walls. "Do you hear it?"

I stood and went to the window. In the distance, I saw a darkness forming into a funnel. Karina jumped down from her bunk and ran to the window. We were on the fourth floor of the prison, at the very top. In the event of a tornado, people are supposed to go to the basement or take shelter in a ground-floor room. Absent that option, people should take shelter under a heavy desk or piece of furniture and stay away from any windows. My instinct to flee kicked in, but I was locked up. Stuck. No guards were there to help, because they had taken shelter on a lower level. So there we were, on the top floor of a building with a tornado forming right in our line of sight.

"Should we get under the bed?" my roommate asked. We looked at each other, then the little bunk bed. We couldn't both fit. The lights flickered on and off.

I was transfixed, staring at the funnel heading directly toward us. My face was just inches from the glass when debris flew by the window.

"Was that a fender?" Karina asked, her voice high with alarm. She jumped back as far as she could from the window. Car parts flew by as the funnel got bigger, the whistling louder. The prison's big institutional laundry baskets floated by the window, spinning in the air almost elegantly. The funnel drew closer. Because we couldn't hide or even cover ourselves, I wasn't tempted to run away. I just watched—eyes wide. My life didn't flash before my eyes like I was in a movie or book. But I didn't know if we were going to live or die.

Is this how it's going to end? I wondered. I'd been told I would die in prison, and I knew I was at peace with the Lord. *But like this?*

It was 5:25 p.m. The funnel turned and came directly at me, then turned ever so slightly. The ceiling shook. The lights flickered off and on again, then went out for good. Our walls cracked. All the toilets began flushing at once, really fast, over and over again. Dust burst through the vents, falling on us. In the darkness, I saw little electrical sparks illuminating the faces of the other trapped women. I could also see them in another wing of the building. Though I couldn't hear them, I saw their mouths open in fear.

By this time, I didn't hear the whistle or the stereotypical sound of a freight train. All I heard were the guttural moans and screams of trapped women in the path of destruction. All I could hear was the screaming. The wailing.

We were still alive, at least for now. Having survived the initial impact of the tornado, would we die of fire? I'd never seriously feared for my life until that moment, when death seemed to taunt us in our little locked cages. Sparks flew. Electrical wires fell. Surely, I thought, the guards will come and help us escape. But they didn't.

When you are living in the outside world, part of being in a storm is checking on the news and reading the up-to-the-second weather reports about where the tornado is—and most important, is not. It's comforting to look at the news, to see the videos, to hear the tired voices of the people cleaning up uprooted trees. Then you can go back to your own life, secure in the knowledge that the danger has passed. But we couldn't hear the weather reports. We couldn't check Twitter. We couldn't go into the atrium and turn on the television. We couldn't even talk to anyone on the outside who could tell us about what happened. We were locked in cells, some of which had four inches of water as the sparks flew and wires dangled.

Over an hour had passed without any word.

"Should we lie down?" Karina asked. It seemed weird to recline on our cots in that chaos, but we needed rest. We did just that, but rest didn't come.

"Everyone okay?" A guard eventually came in and walked through the dark outside the cells. He had a flashlight that briefly illuminated the space. Of course, it was a ridiculous question. No one was okay. Though the screams had subsided, women were still crying.

"Let us out," people cried from their wet cells, but the guard kept going, making his rounds. When he left, the heavy door locked behind him.

Karina looked at me, disappointed. "At least he could've given us food."

"Well, you can thank me for saving your life," I joked, "because I have some ramen noodles in my locker. We can use some of this water to make it edible." Using the bags of tuna I had, I created some pretty good pasta salad. I was trying to calm Karina down by making jokes and survival food. Later that evening, they opened up the food trap in the gigantic doors and dropped through half-frozen sandwiches.

The women continued to cry. All night long. By this point, I wondered if they were still scared or if they were in despair over being abandoned in the direct path of the tornado. I closed my eyes and tried to sleep, but I couldn't tune out their calls. Even in the middle of the night, some prisoners—perhaps in areas harder hit—were still hollering, "Somebody help me."

Their cries came up through the vents.

The next day, the guards let us out for really quick showers but we immediately had to go back to our rooms. Televisions hung off the walls by their cords, some cell floors were cracked, and debris littered the area. It was still raining, and water came in through the newly opened cracks. Part of a roof had been ripped off in a different area of the prison, and part of the external fence had been damaged. Other women were placed into our unit and slept in the common areas for weeks. My family was worried sick about me, since the phone lines and computers were down and they wouldn't let us leave our cells to communicate.

The prison sent out a press release saying that the administration building had been damaged, but that the prison areas were unscathed. The truth, however, was far more grim. For eight days, we lived in "crisis mode," which meant—once again—I had to rely on my faith to get me through.

∞∞∞∞∞∞∞∞

Despite all the damage that was done to the prison during the tornado, video chat came to Aliceville the following month. For the first time we would be able to see people outside the prison as we talked to them on the phone. I'll never forget the day we were able to sit down in front of a screen and see our loved ones in the outside world. No long journeys, no strip searches, no awkwardness required. Everybody was just going crazy to be able to see their families' faces. Some of them were in other countries. Others hadn't seen their families since they were incarcerated. What a joy it was to witness them seeing their families for the first time in decades.

When it was my turn, I gasped when I saw the faces of my grandson Christopher and my great-grandson DJ for the first time. There was nothing like seeing them move and respond to me. In that dark place, I clung to the hope of seeing them on a regular basis. We had to schedule our video chat sessions in advance, since we had to share the computers with all the others.

However, sometimes events would happen that prohibited me from making my preappointed time. The fire alarms were really sensitive, for example, and would trigger emergency responses. Or, if other women got into fights, we'd have to go into our cells. When circumstances stopped us from seeing our families, we had no way of telling them why we didn't show up. I hated to imagine my kids sitting expectantly in front of a computer screen, hoping to see their mother . . . and me not showing up. Yet it was still much better than not having it as an option. Video visits cost six dollars for a twenty-five-minute session, and we were allowed to have only three sessions scheduled at a time, four days in advance. Usually, I managed to do it twice a week, and sometimes even three times. The cost added up, but that didn't matter. I would work around the clock if it meant seeing my family.

The funny thing about video chat was that soon I was speaking to a lot more people than just my family.

Chapter 12

When I arrived in Aliceville, my first case manager was Ms. Benton, who was wonderful. When she left, I was assigned to Aubrey Collins, who was all about his work. He had many duties, including handling the paperwork for releases, helping with relocation, collaborating with federal courts, handling probation, and making living arrangements. He was known for his compassion—for example, he helped prisoners who were trying to transfer closer to home—so everyone wanted to be on his caseload.

One of his duties was to consider media or speaking requests and grant written approvals, of which I always kept a copy. Though everyone had video chat access, certain interviews required permission and advance approval. There was no guarantee that prisoners could earn this privilege. Thankfully, Mr. Collins was very supportive of me. "I'm on Team Alice," he said. He told me that he saw something in me. "I've seen you go the extra mile at the chapel, so I want to go the extra mile for you."

Shortly after we gained access to video chat, I started to receive requests to speak at events or on a platform via video, and whenever I received such a request, he went by the book. The coordinators were Topeka Sam and Brittany Barnett, point people with whom Mr. Collins worked to vet and approve these events. There were certain things I couldn't say during these conversations—for example, I wasn't allowed to speak negatively about the prison or speculate on topics that didn't directly relate to my freedom.

"Stay focused on the goal," he told me, "and your freedom."

And so I did. It took a lot of time, but he made it possible for me to speak to various outlets in ways that other prisoners couldn't.

I'll never forget it.

Speaking opportunities like these continued to open doors for me to share my story. In many ways, the video chat technology couldn't have come at a better time for me: with the Obama Clemency Project in high gear, sharing my voice with the outside world could be a powerful tool for educating others and hopefully winning freedom.

Though my image had already appeared to a nationwide audience in print publications, in 2016 my voice would finally be heard. It would be a big year for my family and me as we fought for my freedom. In March, my daughters went to Washington, DC, for a Justice Roundtable discussion hosted by the social justice activist Nkechi Taifa at which they made a speech advocating for my clemency. In June, there was a first-ever radiothon, in which I got to speak from prison on prison reform. Mr. Collins liked that I could speak directly about my experiences and hopefully change some of the stereotypes about prison.

The following month, I spoke via video chat at Hunter College in Manhattan. Eventually I spoke to students at New York University, Yale University, and the University of Washington, as well as at Google and YouTube events via video chat. I was delighted to be able to tell my story and—in a way—briefly escape those walls.

Meanwhile, Brittany Barnett arranged for my sisters to participate in a #Cut50 event in Washington called Home for the Holidays. #Cut50, a bipartisan effort to reduce the number of people in our prisons and jails, took part in a vigil outside the White House with many other family members of prisoners who were seeking clemency.

Through their advocacy, they began to realize that there were many people in the same circumstance I was in. As my family became more public and started participating in rallies and vigils, they were stunned to learn just how many first-time offenders had been locked up in cages. On August 3, 2016, President Obama issued the most sentence commutations in the history of this nation: 214 people would be going home to rejoin their families. Once again, I wasn't one of them.

Many of the people on that list, to my surprise, didn't really even fit the criteria: some hadn't served ten years, others had gun charges. And very few women had been granted clemency. Not to mention that Attorney General Holder had estimated ten thousand clemencies, and we were way below that number. Obama was on his way out of office, but I still had a chance.

On the other side of the bars, America was experiencing one of the more bitter presidential campaigns in memory. Soon the nation would find out if the next president would be former secretary of state Hillary Clinton or the businessman Donald Trump. When the others were watching television, they usually weren't tuned in to news channels. But a couple of us camped out in front of a television and made sure it was tuned to news stations to keep abreast of current events. I made sure to watch the debates.

Sometimes I couldn't believe my ears and eyes. Those debates were just crazy. *What's going to happen tonight?* I wondered as the moderator introduced the candidates. I'd never really watched debates before I was put in prison. But politics, for us, wasn't just some sort of fun drama playing out on television screens. The millions of votes that Americans cast throughout the nation would have a direct effect on the thousands of people languishing behind bars. It was too high stakes to be entertaining. My ears were tuned in to hear what they said about criminal justice reform.

Most of the women I knew believed Clinton would be more likely to continue with the clemency that President Obama had started. They feared Trump would be less charitable toward prisoners, especially those convicted of drug-related crimes. I had no idea. The Republicans claimed to be tough on crime, and one of the most popular chants at Trump's rallies was "Lock her up!" This was referring to Hillary Clinton specifically, but most of Trump's rhetoric included language that indicated he was interested in putting people behind bars, not freeing them. Though the general anticipation of the nation was that Clinton would be elected president, there were no guarantees she'd be interested in clemency either.

I tuned in to every debate, but there was so much drama happening that I just couldn't keep track of. For example, at the height of the campaign, the rapper Kanye West made a controversial statement at the MTV Video Music Awards: "And yes, as you probably could have guessed by this moment, I have decided in 2020 to run for president." Apparently Kanye had a history of making controversial political statements.

I'd heard the name Kanye West, because people would walk around singing his songs in prison, the tunes coming out of the headphones they incorrectly wore around their necks. When he criticized Trump, however, it wasn't relevant to my life. What did I have in common with two of the biggest celebrities in the world?

Absolutely nothing.

I was focused on getting clemency through President Obama's program. Two years after the initiative was announced, the White House urged the public to get in all the petitions or they'd never have time to evaluate them all. In this batch, there were 6,195 petitions, and mine was one of them. Again.[1]

As we waited to see who would be granted clemency, the unthinkable happened. On the night of November 8, 2016, we gathered around the television to watch the results. The women were excited to see Clinton become the first woman president. Maybe she'd help them get out, they figured. President Obama's list of clemency recipients had been depressingly low on women.

---

[1] "Clemency Initiative," United States Department of Justice, Office of the Pardon Attorney, December 11, 2018, https://www.justice.gov/pardon/clemency -initiative.

But as we watched, the hope began to drain out of many people's faces.

"What in the world?" someone said as the map kept lighting up red, indicating that Trump had won those states. We thought we were getting ready to see history being made—and we were right. Instead of the first woman president, we watched an outsider earn his spot in the Oval Office. By ten o'clock, it was obvious that Trump would be our next president, causing moans and groans from the other women. When the television went off at its predetermined time, we listened to the returns on the radio.

Then we heard the announcement.

"Donald Trump has just been elected president of the United States," said the voice over the radio. The women started reacting inside their cells. "We can't *believe* it," I heard, followed by, "Do you believe Trump is our new president? Oh, Lord, what's gonna happen now?"

But I was not in despair. I did know it took a long time for presidents to acclimate to the position, and prisoners were not usually at the top of their priority lists. So before I went to sleep that night, I prayed. "God, please help the newly elected president, Donald John Trump, remember us in prison."

As it turned out, Kanye seemed to have a change of heart toward the president-elect. "I told y'all I didn't vote, right? But if I would've voted, I would've voted for Trump," he said at a concert. A month later, he went to visit the president-elect at Trump Tower, saying, "I feel it is important to have a direct line of communication with our future president if we truly want change."

Though I didn't know it at the time, this "direct line" to the White House would hold the key to my future.

◇◇◇◇◇◇◇◇◇◇

In December 2016, I wrote an article for CNN that appealed directly to President Obama, making my case in public in the hopes that he would see it and grant me clemency. Would this work?

On December 20, 2016, the prison called three names over the loudspeaker to go to the lieutenant's office: LaShonda Hall, Jean Means, and Alice Johnson. Previous clemency recipients had been alerted in precisely this way, and all three of us were up for clemency. I'd even helped Ms. Means file her papers, since she had been there even longer than I had. We knew that the outgoing President Obama was about to announce another batch.

My heart surged with joy. *This is it!* People looked at us excitedly as we walked past. When we arrived, someone told us to sit down.

"Wait for the executive assistant," we were told. We looked at each other excitedly and held hands that were shaking with joy. This happened to be Tretessa's birthday, so I was thinking what a great gift my clemency would be for her. The others were crying as we waited. After all, this could mean only one thing. One of the lieutenants came out and saw us waiting there. "Hey, Miss Johnson," he said. "You have good news?"

I only smiled.

"Congratulations," he said.

Ms. Williams came in with a folder in her hand and called the first of us back. LaShonda Hall practically ran back. When she came out, her face had fallen. She was crushed. I tried to talk to her, to find out what happened, but she was too devastated to speak.

"Miss Johnson," Ms. Williams said. I went back. "I have a media request for you."

"Is that all?"

"Yes. Sign here if you want to do it." I signed the paper with an arm as stiff as wood. I felt numb as I heard her call Jean back.

Jean, however, had received a commutation. Her sentence was reduced from life to thirty years, which meant she had five years left to do. On that day, President Barack Obama pardoned seventy-eight people and granted commutations to one hundred and fifty-three individuals. I was not one of them.

I was happy for Ms. Means, but calling three people down when there was only one commutation granted was unintentionally insensitive. Ms. Williams was a kind woman, and she meant no harm. But I went back to the cell in a stupor, sat in a chair, and started rocking. My friend Mae Mae came in, saw me, and burst into tears along with me. Then my close friend Cristie came in, kneeled beside me, and held my hand. "I'm so sorry, Miss Alice."

My friends were shocked because they'd never seen me so distraught. That was the hardest day, because—just for a moment—I questioned God's plan for me. Had I misunderstood God's will for my life?

Catina had previously described me as a phoenix, the mythical bird that rises from the ashes. During this time, I remembered the comparison: before the phoenix can rise from the ashes, it has to be burned all the way out.

Well, I had burned all the way out. There can't be a resurrection without death.

We had a prayer circle that met every night at nine o'clock. That night, I explained to my friends what happened. I told them that God never said we wouldn't have trials and tribulations, but He promised that He was enough to overcome them.

I was devastated, but I led the prayer anyway. "I know He hasn't brought me this far to leave me," I told them. "I will not stop."

The Word of God tells us that we walk by faith, not by sight. At that time, I couldn't see the way, but I set my faith and said, "I am not turning back."

On January 6, a flurry of denied commutations was announced, and a collective wailing went through the prison. Since I had not received one of the letters, I assumed I hadn't been denied. Everyone in the family was thrilled. I'd missed the guillotine.

However, on January 9, when I called home, Catina asked me, "Mama, are you okay?"

"I'm fine, why?"

"Have you talked to your lawyer?"

"No," I said.

"Tretessa looked through the list and it shows you were denied on January 6."

I was silent for so long, she asked me, "Are you okay? Are you okay?"

I wasn't. I called Marcia Shein and she apologized. "I'm so sorry, Alice honey. The whole office is hurt over this."

"Why does this keep happening?" I asked.

"The only thing I can think of is that it had something to do with the prosecutor," she said. "When a prisoner's in the final stages of clemency consideration, the pardon attorney bounces it back to the prosecutor. Maybe that was where it stalled."

In prison, when you're serving a lifetime sentence, you rarely experience a sense of running out of time, since time is the only thing you have—and plenty of it. However, on this day, January 9, 2017, I felt a surge of panic. Only eleven days before Obama left office for good.

I called Catina back.

"Stuart Canale might be the weak link," I told her. I then explained Marcia's theory about how the prosecutor possibly played a role in denying my clemency.

"Why would he do that?" she asked. "I'm going to find out what's going on."

"You don't have much time," I told her. President Obama was going to make one more clemency announcement before he left office. I had one more shot.

She called Mr. Canale the next morning.

"I'm Catina Johnson," she explained when she got Canale on the phone, "and I need to talk to you about my mom."

Mr. Canale was taken aback. He told her that she was the first person from any case he'd tried to reach out to him in this way. "How is your mother?" he asked kindly. "And your siblings?"

They talked on the phone for a while, exchanging pleasantries and updates. He acted like they were good friends, as if he had forgotten how terribly he had treated my family the last time he'd seen them.

Then Catina got straight to the point. "Do you have anything against my mother?" she asked. "She's done her time, and she's served it well."

"Every time her petition came across my desk, I simply stamped 'Denied' on it," he said. "I'd just been going by what I knew of Alice twenty years ago."

"But she's changed so much," Catina told him. "She's in the newspapers, she's given interviews, she has lectured about drugs and prison to students at Yale."

"I've never heard any of this," Mr. Canale said. "As far as I know, she never admitted guilt or even apologized for what she's done."

That took Catina by surprise. This was information that should've been included in the clemency materials. But she pressed even further. "Can I come by to show you proof of how much she's changed?"

"Sure," he relented. "You can do that. But I want to see an apology from her in writing."

That evening, we talked on the phone; Catina's voice was full of hope. "Mama, he didn't know about any of your good behavior and all of the people you have helped in prison. You have to write him a letter," she said. "And make it apologetic."

I couldn't believe what I was hearing. How could he claim that I never took responsibility for my actions, since I've never denied the role I played in relaying information between drug dealers? I'd admitted it, I'd apologized. Repeatedly.

"Well, do it one more time," she said. "And make it sound good."

I took a deep breath and began what could've been one of the most important letters I'd ever write. When I got to the end of it, I said a quick prayer and emailed it to Catina. She printed it and added it to her stack of materials.

When Patricia heard of this, even though she was three hours away, she immediately got in the car, picked up Dolores, and they drove to be with Catina. That afternoon, all three of them went to see Mr. Canale. Catina walked right into his office and laid all the materials on his desk. The stack included letters from my wardens, progress reports, clear-conduct reports, news articles in which I had admitted the crime and showed remorse, and information on various awards.

"I hope you can tell from these documents that my mother deserves to be free," she said. Then she added, "I've also included a letter of apology from her."

They watched as his eyes moved down the paper, which he flipped over on his desk when he got to the bottom of it. They were silent as he began reading the next. "You'll see all the good things she's done in prison," Catina said as he began to thumb through the papers. "She's not a threat to anyone."

"I never knew any of this," he said. Catina smiled at her aunts. "These documents are actually very impressive."

"You'll sign the papers saying you had a change of mind?" Catina asked.

"Well, you've changed my mind. But you'll need to talk to my boss and get him to sign the letter. Call his secretary and make an appointment to see him."

"Obama's leaving office in a week," Patricia protested.

"He's a busy man," he said. "You can't just show up and expect to see him."

When they left Mr. Canale's office, they excitedly emailed me and I contacted Amy and members of my legal team—Jennifer, Brittany, and Marcia—and explained the situation.

"Do you think your family can get the signature of the US attorney?" Jennifer asked, taking the lead. "That's all we need, but we need it by Friday."

"I do," I said, though it was already Wednesday evening. Though I wasn't sure if they could pull it off, I had to speak in faith. I knew they'd do everything in their power. My team told me they would try to stall the White House, which was eager to release the final batch of clemency names. They surely wanted to do this far enough before the inauguration to enjoy the press and praise that comes with such an act of goodwill. Plus, I thought of all the people in prison who were so eager to read their name on that list—myself included. Jennifer told her contact at the White House that they had to wait on their announcement, because they'd be adding one more name to the list. "It would be a grave miscarriage of justice for you to release that list without Alice's name on it."

They agreed to wait, but told her, "Get us that form, and now."

As everyone in DC stood by, my family called the office of the US attorney, Edward Stanton, to get an appointment for the next day.

"He's going out of town tomorrow afternoon," his secretary said, cheerily. "But I'd be happy to work you in when he returns."

"That's not going to work," Catina said. "We need an appointment for tomorrow."

"He's not here," the secretary said, her voice firm.

Catina hung up the phone and told my family the bad news. Would my clemency be thwarted because of logistics? It didn't seem like the way this story should end, in paperwork, missed opportunities, and an empty blank line.

That evening, my family gathered to figure out what to do. "We won't take no for an answer anymore," Julius said.

Because of Coria's involvement in law enforcement, she was able to get the phone number for the US attorney's dad. She wrote it on a piece of paper and held it up to the family.

"Should we call him?" Patricia asked. It was late. Coria glanced at the clock on the wall, then at Julius. He nodded. This was no time for southern manners.

I imagine her voice was full of desperation when she finally connected with him. To his credit, the US attorney's father didn't convey irritation at being called so late and even assured them he'd do all he could do to help. Also, Patricia figured out she'd been in the same sorority as Stanton's wife. All the way until midnight, they were on the telephone, calling everyone they knew who might even tangentially know this US attorney.

But there was one more part of their plan, a huge gamble. Bright and early, they went down to Stanton's office to get an audience with him. They hoped he might go into the office before leaving on vacation. They also hoped the secretary would give them a chance, that Stanton wouldn't be super annoyed at this large family filling up his lobby without an appointment, and that they'd leave with a letter from him notifying the pardon attorney that he had reversed his decision. Even with so many unknown variables, they still strategized on who would say what once they got his attention: each sibling would say something on my behalf, making a specific point, taking turns. They were going to be my voice. But before they went, Dolores grabbed the obituary of my mama and put it on the package of information they were bringing. As they walked out the door, Patricia said, "We're taking Mama with us."

The secretary looked at this gaggle of people, then back at her computer screen. "You said you have an appointment?" she asked, her voice full of skepticism. "When did you make this . . . appointment?"

"It was late last night," Coria said. After speaking to Stanton's dad, she *felt* like she had an appointment, but facts are stubborn things.

"I'm sorry," the secretary said, her voice barely containing her irritation. "We don't have you down, and he's not here. Maybe I can let you see his assistant?"

"No," Patricia said. "We need to see Stanton."

The secretary watched helplessly as my family sat down in the chairs in the waiting room. No one said a word. The room was in a nondescript government building, and they could stay there forever if they had to.

A few minutes later, Mr. Canale strode through the office, pausing only briefly to take in the scene. The half-frozen expression on his face, according to my family, was priceless.

Didn't the office secretary tell you the US attorney was going out of town? Didn't I tell you to get an appointment? What on earth is wrong with you people?

But it never occurred to my family to leave. Mr. Canale strode purposefully past them, as if they were furniture around which he needed to navigate. But my family sat and sat some more. Then a miracle happened. The US attorney walked through the door. Before his secretary had the opportunity to explain how much my family had imposed, they stood up and greeted him.

Coria spoke first: "I talked to your dad last night about our situation. Do you have a minute to talk?" He stopped, took in the situation, looked at the secretary's apologetic face, and then spoke.

"Five minutes," he sighed, "but not a second more."

My family followed him into his office. Though each had prepared a little speech, they didn't have time to do their full presentations. Dolores gave him an entirely new copy of all the materials Catina had given to Mr. Canale earlier—just in case he hadn't passed them along. Mr. Canale sat right there in the room, silent.

Patricia took the lead.

"Yesterday, we talked to Mr. Canale, who told us he hadn't heard of all the good things that Alice has been doing in prison." She looked at Mr. Canale. "Thank you for explaining the process of how Alice got denied. In your own words, you yourself admitted that all of her activities were impressive."

She spoke the whole time. You could've heard a pin drop. Patricia said she made eye contact with everyone, who looked back at her encouragingly. Though to this day she can't recall exactly what she said, my siblings assured me she covered all the bases.

She made sure they knew that because President Obama was leaving office, they needed to act now. She ended it with, "As a family, we are so sorry this happened. And, also as a family, we will make sure this will never happen again."

For at least five minutes, they had the ear of the man who could change everything. "All we need is for you to write a letter saying you have reversed your opinion," Patricia said. "And we need it as soon as possible. People at the White House are standing by."

Their five minutes were up, so they stood, shook his hand, and thanked him profusely for his time.

On Friday morning, everyone was in an excited mood but went their separate ways. They were proud of themselves for what they had accomplished.

Coria's phone rang. It was the US attorney's office.

"Due to newly discovered evidence," Stanton read from the letter, "I recommend clemency under President Obama."

Coria burst into tears. "He wrote it," she said to each family member when she called them.

"She's not going to die in prison!" Patricia screamed out.

"We need to have a party," Coria said, sniffling back her tears. "A big welcome-home party, right here." They were dancing and crying and shouting for joy. Immediately Jennifer got in touch with her contacts at the White House and asked them to add me to the list.

January 13, 2017, seven days before Obama left office. My family had done it, just in time. I would be free.

When Amy heard this, she said, "This will be the cherry on the top of this clemency project!"

My family had done everything they could do, becoming a remarkable team of advocates. The team that was fighting for me was dubbed Team Alice. Jennifer ("the general"), Brittany, and Marcia tag-teamed to do everything they could do on the legal side of things, along with Amy, who was calling all of her contacts. Jennifer had been sending notes to the White House, drawing up new clemency petition, and begging the Obama administration to hold off.

"The US attorney's office is going to overnight you the reversal letter," she told them.

"The US attorney letter is all we need," they said.

My legal team vowed to fight around the clock until the last list came out, but—improbably—it looked like we were about to pull this thing off.

On January 19, 2017, President Obama granted his last commutation of sentences. Everyone was waiting on pins and needles. But I was not on the list. The final list.

Eventually I had to break the news to the team, who had been working through sleepless nights. I called Jennifer. Her first words to me were "Are you on it?"

"No," I said.

She began crying. Then I had to break the news to Brittany, Amy, and Marcia.

After I finished with the last disappointed call, I hung up the phone. I couldn't move. I just stood there with my hand on the receiver. Frozen. Devastated. Then I took a deep breath. No one around me knew of the drama that had taken place, and I didn't want to answer any questions. I squared my shoulders and walked back to my cell.

He was still in office. President Obama would be leaving in less than twenty-four hours, but I held on to the hope that someone had managed to get through to him. We'd done everything we were supposed to do, and my family had come through. Maybe I'd be the last clemency he would grant before he walked out—the lone person on the list.

I knew they'd gotten through to the White House.

Refusing to give up hope, I would not accept the fact that Obama had rejected me for clemency until he left office for good. The next day, I sat in front of the television in the common room, watching the inauguration. When Obama turned and waved good-bye to the crowd, my heart sank.

Finally I could see the truth.

I'd officially and undeniably been left behind.

Chapter 13

⌒

Where do I go from here?

As promised, President Donald John Trump was a different kind of president. The inaugural song that he danced to said it all: "My Way." After he appointed Jeff Sessions to the position of attorney general, Sessions issued an order that surprised everyone. Though a consensus had grown between political parties that the criminal justice system needed to be reformed, Sessions ordered that prosecutors pursue the toughest possible charges against criminal defendants like me. It even included more mandatory minimum sentences. This instruction left those of us who were sentenced during the failed era of the War on Drugs reeling in despair. Far from being a war on drugs, it had turned into a war on families that separated people from their loved ones for decades—and too often, even for life.

Even with all the drama that had taken place in the US attorney's office in Memphis, I still believed that I would one day walk out of prison. I had gotten the US attorney, Edward Stanton, on my side, and he had become convinced I needed to be set free. A flame had been lit that we were going to continue to fan.

Now that the door was open to us, my daughter Catina called the US attorney's office the day after Obama left office. When Stanton's secretary answered the phone, my daughter identified herself.

"The whole office was pulling for Alice," the secretary said.

"Do you think your boss would support a sentence-reduction motion for my mother?" she asked.

"Get us a motion and we can try again to get your mother free."

"Woo-hoo!!!" Catina screamed as she hung up the phone.

My clemency attorney Marcia Shein prepared a sentence-reduction motion and filed it on my behalf. Less than two weeks later, we were shocked to learn that Edward Stanton was resigning as US attorney. We saw it on the news that February 28 would be his last day in office. But we'd gone too far and fought too hard to give up by then. I was no longer parking my hope on a man—because I'd finally learned that hope is *not* a man.

I was scheduled to speak at New York University the last week of January 2017. When I accepted the invitation, I'd hoped I would be speaking as a free woman who had been granted clemency. Instead I spoke of the heartbreak that I, along with thousands of other prisoners, was feeling after having been left behind. The first platform I had spoken at via video visit had been orchestrated by the National Council for Incarcerated and Formerly Incarcerated Women and Girls at Hunter College. Andrea James was the president of that group, and Topeka Sam was the national organizer. My final university speaking engagement from prison was through the same council.

In the spring of 2017, Malika Saada Saar, the senior counsel on civil and human rights at Google, invited me to speak at a Google-hosted YouTube summit on criminal justice reform. Malika first heard me speak through a YouTube platform at a #cut50 Clemency Now event in November 2016 that was being hosted by Google in DC. Little did I know the role that technology and Google would play in my fight for freedom.

Jake Horowitz with MIC attended the Google summit and was so moved by my words that he sought out a way to connect with me to do a video op-ed. Google connected Jake to Topeka, who had access to contact me and coordinate video visits. Topeka told me that Jake was interested in my doing a video op-ed, but it would be months before I would hear anything about it again.

Kendall Ciesemier arrived at MIC the first week of October 2017, and Jake reupped the email chain. After a date was set for me to do the video op-ed, Jake organized a time for Topeka to come to MIC to test the technology.

On October 16, 2017, I called Topeka to find out how I would be introduced to begin the video op-ed. That's when I discovered that it would not just be me speaking into a camera, but a news reporter would actually be interviewing me. This was a problem, because conversations with any kind of journalist required special approval from the prison. Topeka and I both knew that though I'd been previously been interviewed via video visit, I had never sat down with an actual reporter. When I spoke of my concern to her, Topeka said that she had just found those details out that day and understood if I couldn't do it. She told me that she would let MIC know. I told her to wait and I'd get back to her.

I went back to my cell and pulled out all the approvals, including the blanket approval I had received to speak on various platforms via video visit. I reviewed again the stipulation that said I had approval to do video visit interviews as long as I didn't speak negatively about the prison. I felt good about what I had in writing; the only problem was that the staff member who had given me the approval was on leave. Who there would give me permission? Plus, what if they said no?

I couldn't take the chance.

I prayed, as the possible consequences of not getting permission for this ran through my mind. I thought of Queen Esther in the Bible, who made the decision to go before the king to save lives in spite of the fact that it was against the law to go before the king unannounced. She said, "If I perish, I perish." Then she touched the heart of the king. I thought about all the times in my life that I had fought against injustice. Was not my family worth fighting for? Was not my life worth fighting for? Were the other prisoners, whose faces no one might ever see, worth fighting for? In life, sometimes you have no choice but to fight.

I went downstairs and made a phone call. "Topeka, I have decided to do it."

When I told my friends what I had decided, they were not thrilled. "Miss Alice, you know what could happen if you do this?"

"What if this is my last chance to be free?" I replied. They had no answer to that. Plus, they knew they couldn't change my mind.

The next morning was October 17. I got up early so that Cindy, one of my friends in the unit—who happened to be a beautician and a former beauty pageant contestant—could fix my hair. I wanted one of those swept-back styles reminiscent of a 1960s secretary. When she finished, she had achieved the perfect look: it was pinned up with a little sprig coming down on the side.

At 8:00 a.m., the shift changed, and the next officer came on duty. I went back in my room and laid my uniform out on my bed and made sure my boots looked good (even though the reporter wouldn't be able to see them). I wanted the confidence that I looked as good as possible, even down to my feet. When I heard the officer making his morning rounds, I looked out my cell. I couldn't believe my eyes. Our regular officer had not come in, and the person who was working his post for the day was none other than my unit manager. Yikes! A former member of the military, he was absolutely no-nonsense, constantly walking the unit and making sure that everything was in order.

My heart raced.

If he saw me on that phone with lights and cameras as a backdrop, it was not going to be good. What bad timing!

I pulled out my MP3 player and put on "Fight Song" by Rachel Platten. As I listened to the lyrics—"I may only have one match, but I can make an explosion"—I felt a burst of adrenaline. "Take back my life song," I sang as I danced and twirled around my cell. "I still gotta lot of fight left in me."

The call was set for 10:00 a.m., and I had precisely twenty-five minutes to be on a video visit.

When I told my friends that our unit manager was on duty as

our officer, their faces grew ashen. And so they hatched a plan to help me. They were going to take turns keeping him engaged in conversation in the officer's station. When one finished talking to him, another would enter the office and speak to him. Another friend stood outside the room where I would be talking to the reporter via video visit and promised to flash a signal if I needed to abruptly abort the call. Another friend stood in the corner near where I was making the call and prayed the entire time. Everyone was still very upset about my being passed up for clemency and wanted to help me.

I took a deep breath, sat down at the computer terminal, and logged in. Kendall popped onto the screen. Just as I expected, bright lights and cameras were directed toward me. Kendall briefed me on how the interview would flow and said, "Feel free to skip a question if it makes you feel uncomfortable." But nothing did. I felt such a sweet peace envelop me. I looked into the eyes of the camera and imagined that I was looking into the eyes of a single person. I felt a strong connection to my unseen audience.

"My name is Alice Marie Johnson," I began. "I am a sixty-two-year-old mother, grandmother, and great-grandmother. In less than two weeks, on October 31, will mark my twenty-first year of confinement in federal prison." The reporter stopped to ask questions, like what prison life was like, how it felt to see my family while I was locked up, and so forth.

As my answers flowed out, it felt like I could bare my soul and tell of my pain, shame, disappointments, and even triumphs. No written article could articulate who I was better than my own voice.

I told her what a close family member had told me about how

sad it was to visit me in prison and know I would never rejoin her except as a corpse. She said it was like visiting a gravesite. They could view the place where my body was but could never take me home. I talked about the big moments that I'd missed—the births of grandchildren and great-grandchildren; the deaths of both of my parents and one sister and not being able to attend their funerals. I explained that I had been active while in prison and maintained clear conduct the entire time. I told her definitively that I was not a risk to society. When Kendall asked me to define who I really was, I answered in this way: "The real Miss Alice is a woman who has made a mistake. If I could go back in time and change the choices I made, I would. But I can't. I have not allowed my past to be the sum of who I am." And finally, I made a plea to America: "Please wake up, America, and help end this injustice. It's time to stop overincarcerating your own citizens."

"Thank you, Miss Alice," the reporter said. Right before my twenty-five minutes were up, my friend flashed me a panicked signal. The unit manager was walking up to the window to peek in. I quickly hung up without even saying goodbye. With six seconds to spare, it was done. Come what may, the die was cast.

Kendall later revealed to me that she felt deeply the presence of God while interviewing me. She said it was unlike any story she'd ever heard and she sensed that something bigger was going on while speaking with me. Kendall reached out to my daughter Tretessa and asked her to send family photos. Topeka constantly updated me on what was happening.

The video was scheduled to drop on Thursday, October 19, but

MIC realized that the audio of the video visit hadn't recorded properly. They had to use the audio from the camera that was filming Kendall asking the questions. They told me that the audio wouldn't sync because they were at different "bit rates." I didn't understand anything they were saying, but I knew it wasn't good. I'd gone to so much effort and had taken so much risk, this interview had to be published. It was now or never. Thankfully, Abu Zafar edited the piece with skill and perseverance. Though a lot of effort had to go into making it work, MIC finally felt it was ready to go.

The video dropped on October 23 and almost immediately started trending. It was as if it had a life of its own. My family and friends were emailing me with numbers. "It's going viral," they gushed. But this scared me. I didn't know what "viral" meant. I was afraid that the video was about to introduce a virus into the internet. Before you think that I was really dumb, you have to realize there was no internet when I came to prison twenty-one years prior, and I wasn't familiar with tech terms.

Celebrities retweeted the video, talk show hosts discussed it on their programs, and even the officers at the prison talked about it. Something amazing was happening. Later that day, I received an email from Amy Povah with a message she forwarded from an attorney named Shawn Chapman Holley. Shawn said that a very rich and famous client of hers wanted to hire her to help me get out of prison, and she wanted to know if I would like for her to do it. She included a number for me to call. There is a country saying: "My drawers didn't touch my behind." That's how fast I was running to call Shawn.

Shawn Holley didn't reveal to me on that first call who this woman was, so I called my daughter and asked her to Google the name "Shawn Holley" and tell me who her clients were. After hearing the list of clients I just knew that rich and famous woman had to be Kris Jenner! Catina wasn't so sure.

"What if it's Kim Kardashian?" she asked. Catina knew Kim because she loved watching *Keeping Up with the Kardashians.*

"Kim who?"

She explained to me how this famous woman had a tender heart for others. I still thought the woman was Kris, but I started searching for pictures and articles about Kim so I would know more about her and what she looked like.

Shawn revealed that my benefactor was Kim Kardashian! She later advised me that she had talked to her client and was now my attorney.

I wrote Kim a thank-you letter expressing my gratitude to her.

Dear Ms. Kardashian,

I am so humbled by what you are doing and have already done on my behalf. When I spoke with attorney Shawn Holley, and she disclosed the name of my benefactor, I had to take the time to process and digest the news that you were the one she had been alluding to.

There are no words strong enough to express my deep and heartfelt gratitude. Ms. Kardashian, you are literally helping to save my life and restore me to my family. I was drowning, and you have thrown me a life jacket and given me hope that this life jacket I'm serving may one day be taken off.

There are defining moments in history that have shaped the destiny of this nation. I believe that we are a part of a defining moment. When Rosa Parks refused to give up her seat on that bus (the same year I was born—1955), that was a defining moment. She was an ordinary woman whose courage ignited and united the heart of America to stand together against a very present evil that could no longer be tolerated. This is so much bigger than either one of us.

I believe that history will record that Kim Kardashian had the courage to take a stand against human warehousing and was a key figure in meaningful criminal justice reform becoming a reality.

A million, trillion thanks! May God's blessing rest upon you and yours.

THE BATTLE IS ON!

Sincerely,

Alice Marie Johnson

October 28, 2017

Shawn didn't have much experience in the federal courts, so she wanted to know who the attorneys were who had been helping me. I gave her the names of Jennifer Turner, Marcia Shein, and Brittany Barnett, who had become a big help.

The video went from viral to super viral. It was the talk of the prison and the talk of the nation. People outside the prison walls were talking about it. Reporters did articles and television segments about me. Mine was one of the most watched videos of the week—celebrities were talking about the video on radio stations. I even got a card from someone I didn't know. The lady told me her fourteen-year-old son was so upset. "Mama, they had a grandmama in prison," he told her. People started calling me America's grandma. People in other countries started weighing in on the broken American criminal justice system. The grandmother serving a life sentence caught international attention. "Who's making the cookies?" someone asked. "They got America's grandma in jail."

People on the outside were asking the people inside there at Aliceville if they knew me. Even the officers were talking about the fact that Kim had retweeted that video. Now the fact that I had made this video certainly wasn't a secret, and I half expected my name to be called over the intercom at any time. I wasn't afraid.

On Monday, October 30, one week after the video had dropped, I danced for a women's abuse program. When I left the chapel, I heard my name being called. I was to report to the lieutenant's office. They had gotten a call from Washington, DC, that there was a possible unauthorized media contact coming from Aliceville. One of the lieutenants wrote a disciplinary report and set a date for me to see the Disciplinary Hearing Office (DHO).

While the lieutenant was talking, my eyes were drawn to a print hanging on the office wall. It depicted an eagle holding branches. The writing on the art said "olive branch." Now, I can't quite remember what else it specifically said, because I felt God was speaking to me, since I'd been raised in the little town of Olive Branch, Mississippi. The poster also had an olive branch being held in the eagle's talons. In the Bible, Noah sent out a dove in search of land after being confined to the ark during the flood. When the dove returned with an olive branch, it indicated dry land. His long ordeal was just about over.

When I went to the DHO, I was handcuffed, my hands behind my back. The officer read the charges against me in such a patronizing way.

"What do you have to say for yourself?

"I had permission," I said.

"You what?" Her face fell. She hadn't expected that. "From who?"

I explained the blanket permission I'd received from Mr. Collins. She was shocked, then furious. "I'll reschedule you to come back next week. Bring the evidence." On November 8, I presented all the papers, but she told me she had done her own investigation and found me guilty.

"I'm sentencing you to fourteen days in the SHU for disciplinary isolation." I also lost my video visitation privileges for six months (this meant that I wouldn't be able to see my family over Thanksgiving, Christmas, or New Year's). "Your time starts today."

◇◇◇◇◇◇◇◇◇◇

My cell was dark and cold, and had one bunk bed and a toilet and a little shower. We had a window made of clear plexiglass with bars on it. Sometimes the prisons used frosted glass so the prisoners couldn't see out of them, so at least they hadn't done that. Because of the increased risk of suicide, they no longer let women be alone in the SHU. My roommate was a Christian woman who had landed in isolation after hand-washing an article of clothing, hanging it out to dry on the sprinkler nozzle in her cell, and causing the sprinklers to go off.

I knew my family didn't know where I was, because I just disappeared. Everyone began to worry as they compared notes about the last time they had talked via video chat or emailed with me. A lack of a response was unlike me. Someone always heard from me. When I missed my scheduled visit with Tretessa via video that had been scheduled for that same day, she got worried and called the prison and discovered I had been put in the SHU.

On that first night, it was hard to fall asleep. My mind raced with all the events that had taken place. I began singing a gospel song, "Amazing Grace," to myself. And then my Jamaican cellmate joined in. Over the course of our isolation, we passed the time by singing gospel songs. Just like in the cotton fields.

The next morning, I awakened early to do my normal prayers. I looked out the small window. On the building near us, I saw an eagle so close. It was staring directly at me. I couldn't believe my eyes. It was perched as if it were at attention, pointing straight at me. I walked to the window and looked at it, but it didn't flinch as I got closer. I stared at that bird for a long time, then fell to my knees to pray. I felt like God—who is sometimes described as an eagle in the Bible—was with me. Just as an eagle watches over her young, I felt that God was watching over me. I felt His gentle presence, and that He knew where I was. I was going to be okay.

The SHU was the most terrible place in an already terrible place. We were locked up twenty-three hours of the day and received one hour of caged recreational activities outdoors. We had just a very small space in which we could walk around inside a cage. And that was just some of the discomforts. The soap they gave us was made from lye, an ingredient to which I was highly allergic. I didn't want to be treated special, but my condition was documented, and I needed sensitive soap. When I went to the recreation department and complained about it to others, they said, "It's not going to do any good to complain to the nurse. She just told us that 'in the old days, people didn't even have soap. You'll make do.'"

When she came the next day, I asked her anyway. She looked at me blankly. "There's nothing I can do." And so I used the few little packs of shampoo until they ran out.

Also, the deodorant they gave us caused my underarms to bleed. When I went to rec and told the other women about the deodorant, they told me no one uses that under their arms but on their feet to keep them soft. It was almost as if I should've known that. So now I didn't have soap or deodorant, and the officers wouldn't give me a different kind. Since I didn't want to stink, I took multiple showers a day. I only had one change of clothes, so I washed my clothes at night using that lye soap, making sure to wring out all the lye, before hanging them up to dry while I slept.

The only book I read in the SHU was the Bible. One day, I opened it up to a random place in the Word, and it opened to Psalm 118. "The stone that the builders rejected has become the chief cornerstone," it read. "This is the Lord's doing and it is marvelous in His sight."

That's when it hit me so hard. This passage, of course, was not written with me in mind. It was about Jesus. But I knew that God was showing me that he was in the business of taking the rejected and shamed, and doing something amazing with them. Jesus was the stone that the builders rejected—and I was rejected for clemency. Jesus became the chief cornerstone. The idea that maybe God would be able to use me for a cornerstone or anything filled me with hope. I wrote that date down in my Bible because I knew I needed to think more about what this could possibly mean.

Being in the SHU turned out to be a time of great peace for me, in spite of the terrible conditions. In fact, I felt like God had used prison to finally answer the question I asked so long ago as a ten-year-old writing poetry: "Who is He?"

Since the video had gone so viral, I could only imagine what was happening on the outside of prison relating to my situation. My roommate said, "Alice, maybe this is a good thing. Here you can put everything out of your head and let everything happen the way it's supposed to unfold." We were supposed to stay down in the hole for fourteen days, but they released us after thirteen. When I went to look out the window, I saw the eagle flying off into the distance.

When I came out of the SHU, just in time for Thanksgiving, things were already in motion. It was as if my one match—the video—had caused an explosion.

Boom!

◇◇◇◇◇◇◇◇◇◇

The publicity surrounding the video got new life when TMZ talked about it on their show and did an article about Kim's mission to free me. They even published the thank-you note I'd written to Kim and included a big picture of me.

"You're on television, Miss Alice!" my friends exclaimed. I came out of my cell and went to the television room. It was surreal to see myself make the news. Everyone watched in silence as my story was told. You might think they would high-five me, or whoop and holler at my appearance. But by this time I was an older woman in this prison for life. They respected me in a way that made it hard for them to treat me casually. I was also on the popular Telemundo show *El Gordo y la Flaca*, which is broadcast to almost every Spanish-speaking country in the world. This made me very popular with the Spanish-speaking women who couldn't even speak English.

From that point forward, I would occasionally appear on shows when they spoke of Kim Kardashian West. My friends couldn't believe this was all happening.

"She's taking your calls?" they'd ask in disbelief.

"She's fighting for me," I'd answer. I called her my war angel, because she was relentless in her fight to free me.

In a comical moment, Tretessa called me, laughing. She had talked to Bryant, who was isolated from the news because he was in prison. "I think the time is finally getting to Mama," he'd told her, worried. "She thinks that Kim Kardashian is trying to get her out of prison." When she told him it was true, he still could hardly believe it.

Kim wanted the best legal team possible to be assembled to work on my case. Shawn Holley, Kim's personal attorney, became the lead attorney for Team Alice. Shawn, well known for her prowess in the courtroom and her ability to effectively argue the toughest cases, quickly familiarized herself with all aspects of my case. Now she was armed with knowledge and dangerous! Jennifer Turner and Brittany Barnett had both successfully prepared clemency petitions for clients who were granted their freedom. They were each highly skilled and knowledgeable about the clemency process and would be the ones to put together legal arguments to present a compelling case for my clemency. Just as important, they were both trusted friends.

While my sentence-reduction motion was pending before Judge Samuel Mays in the Memphis court, a decision was made to bring in a top local attorney. Mike Scholl, a very well known and highly esteemed Memphis lawyer, was hired to take a fresh look at my case and supplement my motion.

Kim had now successfully brought together a team of experts in their fields who were ready to charge ahead in their quest to get me out of prison. She didn't care how my freedom was won, through clemency or the courts—just as long as I was free.

Recess was over, and Team Alice was not playing.

Chapter 14

In December 2017, I felt a surge of hope when President Trump granted clemency to a kosher meatpacking executive named Sholom Rubashkin, a man who faced a twenty-seven-year prison sentence for financial crimes. Since presidents don't normally grant clemencies their first year in office, I felt encouraged that Team Alice would be successful.

I was so thankful that, after all those years of fighting for myself, I had a team fighting for me.

Kim reached out to Ivanka Trump, the daughter of President Trump and one of his top advisers. Since Ivanka had children, we hoped she would be sympathetic to my situation. Ivanka spoke about my case with her husband, Jared Kushner, also a senior adviser to the president. Jared had a natural interest in this topic, ever since his father, the New York developer Charles Kushner, had been sentenced to prison. That meant that Kushner got to see the challenges of the criminal justice system up close and the pain of separation. Ivanka played a major role at the White House working on my behalf. Because she has a strong heart on women's issues, part of her mission in government was to champion causes that strengthen women. I was very blessed to have her working inside the White House on my behalf, because she worked hard to push the needle forward to get Kim in the White House. Throughout this entire fight, she and Kim stayed in contact.

When his father-in-law became president, Jared began working on the Prison Reform and Redemption Act, a bipartisan criminal justice reform bill that aimed to reduce the rate of recidivism of prisoners by preparing them to reintegrate into society more seamlessly. In a series of telephone calls, Kim talked to Jared about my case and tried to figure out how to bring my plight to the attention of the president.

Then, in late December 2017, Ivanka reached out to Kim, and a shudder of excitement ran through all of us. "We need Alice Johnson's clemency packet," she said. Those six words sent our team into a frenzy as they created a brand-new packet to submit. Ivanka said she wanted my packet before they left for the holidays, because they wanted a jump start on reviewing it for the new year.

While all this maneuvering was going on, I tried not to let the excitement paralyze me. I continued to do what I do. I prepared to put on a Christmas play. I heavily relied on Ms. Speight, the secretary in religious services, to help me with all the logistics. When she saw me coming, she'd say, "Okay, Miss Alice, what do you need now?"

The women looked forward to attending the productions, because it helped them keep their minds off missing their families.

For just that moment, I wanted them to be able to imagine walking into a theater in the outside world. I made the sets beautiful and elaborate, so that they felt special. Once again, I elicited their help—props needed to be made, costumes designed, and sets built. Giving them something to do and something to look forward to helped uplift their spirits. Because with all the work, they didn't have time to be depressed.

Anticipation built, and I didn't want to disappoint everyone. Outside guests were allowed to attend this ticketed event, and a record number of people showed up. After the Christmas play, I started gearing up to do my first 100 percent Spanish play.

In April, I was watching the television in prison, which was tuned to CNN. An attorney, Mark Osler, was appearing as a guest. To my surprise, he mentioned me in the interview. He was talking about Jack Johnson, the first black heavyweight boxing champion, for whom many were advocating a posthumous pardon. "If the president pardons *Jack* Johnson, he should also pardon *Alice* Johnson," Osler said. What a surprise to see this man advocating for me on national television!

Also in April, Kanye West tweeted support for the president, which caused the media to go into an absolute frenzy. I believe that Kanye's support of President Trump paved the way for Kim to get the audience with him that she'd been asking for. The very next month, the conversations started picking up in intensity and frequency.

On May 1, 2018, MIC broke the news that Kim was speaking to Kushner, which created another news cycle surrounding me, and the story began to swell. Every news outlet began reporting this development, and people all over America began to pray for my release.

On May 9, the Judiciary Committee approved Kushner's bill, also known as the First Step Act, by a vote of 25–5. This bill aimed to allow ex-offenders to enter back into society in a meaningful and productive way through job training, mental health assistance, and drug treatment.

On May 18, the White House hosted a prison reform summit at which President Trump and Vice President Pence both spoke. The president described the First Step Act as being able to "restore the rule of law, keep dangerous criminals off our street, and help inmates get a second chance on life." Of course, Ivanka and Jared attended this event, as well as other activists like the CNN commentator Van Jones, Topeka Sam, and representatives from the American Conservative Union and Right on Crime. Topeka spoke at this summit and even mentioned my name. Ivanka and Jared made it clear that they were on Team Alice. But most important, President Trump said that if this bill passed through Congress, he would sign it into law.

On May 25, President Trump pardoned Jack Johnson—at the request of the actor Sylvester Stallone. That was a good sign. Was this Kim's chance to get in?

Invigorated by this news, my team continued to fight tirelessly for me. Kim assured me that the second Trump said she could get an audience with him, she would drop everything and go straightaway. We developed a friendship, and my attorneys kept me abreast of everything going on.

I am a fighter, so I was determined to fight that incident report about my punishment following the MIC interview. I did have a blanket approval from staff to do interviews. I appealed to the regional prison authorities, who denied me. Then I appealed to what we referred to as the "supreme court" of prison, which is Central in DC, the ultimate authority. I won, and my record was wiped clean, my clear conduct restored. It was a great lesson for the women with whom I was serving time. I felt that soon I might be walking out of that prison, but I wanted to show them that they could and should fight for themselves. I wanted to give them courage.

With my clear record back in place, the packet was delivered to Jared, who had the legal team at the White House go through my clemency petition. This necessarily included my presentencing report, which contained the estimated amount of drugs I was supposed to have been involved with back in the day. My scarlet letter. They ran my credibility through a sifter, peeling back the layers to show who I really am, instead of who the prosecutor or judge said I was. They saw the person instead of the charges.

It was clear this whole time that Kim wasn't playing any games. She was there to win. And she told me she wouldn't give up until I came home, even if this first effort didn't work. She told me, "I'm not going to stop." The government was now up against a woman who was not going to give up. Make that two women.

My legal team was relentless, working every hour on the clock, preparing paperwork whenever even a crack opened. Kim didn't want to leave any stone unturned. Kim told me she'd explained to Jared Kushner that just like everybody else, I had made choices in my life that I wasn't proud of. Then she explained that rarely do people have to pay as a high price as the one I had been paying. She talked to him on the phone many times over the course of months.

However, it was taking longer than expected to get an audience with the president.

Momentum was growing, so I decided to do what I could do, even though I was behind bars. The article I'd published on CNN back in December 2016 hadn't persuaded President Obama to grant me clemency as I'd hoped. However, I updated it to explain to America why Kim Kardashian West was fighting for me. I began, "Some refer to prison as a place where hope dies. Some days I've found that to be almost right. But at the beginning of my time here I made a pact—that I wouldn't give up hope. Each time that I've come close, God has restored my faith. So when the unlikely voices of Kim Kardashian West and Jared Kushner came together to shine a spotlight on my case, I could only thank God, for He works in mysterious ways."

I went on to describe the incredible outpouring of support I'd received. More than 200,000 people had signed an online petition supporting my release. And it couldn't have come at a better time. Mother's Day was right around the corner, and the very thought of being with my family for the first Mother's Day in twenty-two years was just unbearably exciting.

Also, I explained that the United States leads the world in incarceration rates, containing 5 percent of the global population but one-quarter of the world's prisoners. "Trump has the power to give me a second chance," I wrote. "He truly has the power to change our justice system for the better. I can only continue to be steadfast and hope that he hears me. No matter what happens, I was not built to break. I will keep writing. I will continue to hold my head high and live a productive life either as a free woman or here behind bars. God has shown me my strength."

My article was very well received, and it seemed like people from both parties were coming around to the idea of prison reform. But not everyone in the Trump White House was pulling for my clemency. The newspapers reported that some of the president's top advisers were against my clemency. One called it "unnecessary." Another said he was "disturbed" by the possibility of my clemency. But one thing I knew about the president: he would do whatever he wanted to do.

Then I got a notification that I had a legal call from my attorney and Kim. They told me the date had been set for Kim to have an audience with the president. After a scheduling complication arose, the meeting was delayed. The new date was set: May 30.

"Do you know that that's my birthday?" I asked.

"Get out!" Kim said. "Are you kidding? This is it!"

She was so optimistic, and sure, it made my faith shoot through the roof to hear her excitement. Surely this was a sign. On my birthday, would my gift be freedom? Anyone who said Kim was in this for publicity was completely off base.

I didn't tell anyone that Kim was going to the White House, because I wasn't sure if it was supposed to be a secret. I wasn't going to be the leaker. But early in the morning on the day of my birthday, some women were listening to the *Tom Joyner Morning Show* on the radio.

"Miss Alice!" they screamed. "They're talking about you on

the radio, saying that Kim Kardashian is going to the White House to meet President Trump today!" Everyone was talking about it. Not only in prison, but all over the nation. People had definitely heard Kim's name, but others were hearing my story for the first time. I was so prevalent in the news that someone asked, "Which came first, Alice or Aliceville?"

I had to clean my cell. So I went back and tidied it up. It was my birthday, but I had told everyone I didn't want a party. I grabbed the birthday food I'd made myself the night before (including cheesecake) and sat down in front of the television. The entire prison was abuzz with the news of the impending White House visit. Now that the cat was out of the bag, women in every unit were posted up around the televisions. They didn't want to miss a moment of the unfolding drama taking place involving one of their very own—me . . . a country girl from Olive Branch, Mississippi.

Around lunchtime, a television news show broadcasted a tweet that Kim posted: a message to me. "Happy Birthday Alice Marie Johnson. Today is for you." At the end of her tweet she had included a praying hands emoji. When I saw that, unchecked tears started rolling down my face. What a birthday message and what a surprise!

"We're so excited because they're talking about 'our Miss Alice,'" someone said. No one dared try to change that television. The press was having a field day with Kim's visit. Shawn had been studying and preparing to present an airtight legal defense. Jennifer and Brittany had played devil's advocate as they took her through a series of possible legal questions that might be thrown at her. But Shawn was in her element. The courtroom would be the Oval Office.

It had been seven months since I had caught Kim's attention, in what I could only call a "Godcidence." Over that time, we'd become very close. People frequently asked Kim how she found me. She always responded, "I didn't find Alice, she found me." Yet I knew that God had orchestrated our divine appointment that day. Kim had not been on Twitter for days. How could it be that in the exact moment that she went on Twitter, my face appeared in a tweet? One that someone else retweeted? Whether or not anyone else believes it, I know that God was at work.

I knew that day would culminate in either victory or defeat, an open heart or a closed mind. Earlier that morning, I'd recited Proverbs 21:1: "The king's heart is in the hand of the Lord, like the rivers of water; he turns it wherever he wishes." I prayed that God would turn President Trump's heart toward me.

As I sat at the table eating my birthday food, I saw live footage of Shawn and Kim walking into the White House. Kim was dressed in all black except for a pair of neon yellow translucent pumps. The press was going crazy over her wardrobe, of course. Even from a distance, I could see their steely, determined looks.

After the visit, I received an attorney's call from Brittany and Jennifer, who patched in Kim and Shawn while they were still in the car leaving the White House. They said they thought the meeting had gone really well. Kim said that the president seemed to have a passion for everything that Jared had been trying to do, and she was happy that that conversation was moving forward well. She told me that she thought President Trump really spent the time to listen to her speak about my case. "He really understood," she said, "and I am very hopeful that this will turn out really positive."

In that meeting, the president's eyes were completely opened, and I believe his heart was too, when he was presented with who I am and what I had done in prison. I think it appalled him that a woman who posed no threat to society was wasting away in prison. Even though a celebrity had brought this to his attention, I was no celebrity. I was a human being. My case was worthy to bring before him.

My case had finally made it to the desk of the president.

When I knew that I had done all I could do, I felt a calmness in my soul. I wrote an email to Jennifer, and I said, "We have put forth our very best effort in the natural. Now we are totally dependent on God to put His super- behind our natural, and give us a supernatural victory." I was no longer on pins and needles. I had prayed for Kim to be able to have an audience with the president, the highest authority in the United States. That had happened.

I went to see Chaplain Rachel Floyd, and I discussed all that had been going on. I often sought her out for advice, because we had history. She had been a chaplain at Carswell and had come to Aliceville a few months after I did. She and Chaplain Clay Carroll knew my story, and I relied on them for spiritual encouragement.

"This could be it. If, for any reason, my clemency is granted," I told her, "I want to say goodbye." We talked about me writing a letter to be read to the women in the event of my clemency.

"If you write it, I'll hold it," she said. "If you leave, I'll read it."

And so I sat down and typed out this letter to my church family in prison:

FAREWELL MY BELOVED SISTERS IN CHRIST!

When this letter is read to you, I will no longer be at FCI Aliceville. It is only by the grace of God that I am now a FREE woman. I am greatly humbled by what Jesus has done for me. Without Him, I can do nothing, but with Him there is nothing that I can't do.

I have been so blessed to have experienced firsthand the faithfulness of our Awesome God. These past twenty-one years in prison have been the greatest adventure of my life. So do not mourn for me and think these years have been wasted. God has not allowed anything that I have gone through to be wasted, whether good or bad . . . mistakes or victories . . . tears or laughter . . . delays or denials . . . pain or shame. Through my own suffering, I can now bring comfort. Through my story, your story is being told. Through my face, they will see your face. God has raised up my voice to be your voice . . . and you already know that "NO ONE CAN SHUT MISS ALICE UP!" In all things, in the end God alone gets ALL the glory from my story. HALLELUJAH!

My sisters, I thank you for sharing this journey with me and enriching my life. We have been able to accomplish some amazing things together to advance the kingdom of God. I will never forget you. You have been tattooed on my heart.

I love you! Be blessed and continue to persevere in faith and continue to do the work of the Lord.

Your fellow servant,

Alice Marie Johnson
2018

I signed the letter, put it in an envelope, and sealed it. I wasn't sure if they'd ever get to hear the words on that paper, but I sure hoped they would. And soon.

After the White House meeting, Kim tweeted out a couple of messages:

"I would like to thank President Trump for his time this afternoon. It is our hope that the President will grant clemency to Miss Alice Marie Johnson who is serving a life sentence for a first-time, non-violent drug offense."

Then, she added, "We are optimistic about Miss Johnson's future and hopeful that she—and so many like her—will get a second chance at life." President Trump also tweeted out a photo of him and Kim, with the caption "Great meeting with @KimKardashian today, talked about prison reform and sentencing."

Six days after the meeting, I read an article in the newspaper that said my clemency might happen as soon as the following week. Maybe that's why, the next morning, I didn't believe it when people called me into the television room.

"You gotta come see this," someone hollered from the television room. "You're fixing to go home." By this time, I had been incarcerated for twenty-one years, seven months and six days. It was June 6, 2018. "Are you packed?" another asked. "You better get to it."

I went into my cell, shut the door, looked out the window, and prayed. I didn't need to know all that people were saying about me on the news. I needed quiet. I needed to be alone.

When it was chow time, I went to lunch. It was hamburger day. I just wanted to go do something normal and get away from all the chatter. I sat at a table. I took a bite of my hamburger. Before I could even chew it, I heard my name being called. "Alice Johnson, report back to your unit." I spit out the hamburger into a napkin. Suddenly, I thought about the day I'd been called to the lieutenant's office believing with my whole heart that I'd gotten clemency. It had been a false alarm. Was this?

I walked to my unit, figuring this was another legal call. I was having a lot of those lately. I was thinking about my family, about Kim, about freedom. All the while, people tried to talk to me, telling me I was going home. I shut all that out of my mind and shut out all the noise.

I saw Mr. Holler, who said, "Come on back, you have a legal call." Since this is not how clemency news is normally told, I figured I'd just get another legal update.

"Hello?"

The first voice I heard on the call was Kim's. She was at a modeling shoot, and had just been patched into the legal call.

"Miss Alice . . ."

"Is this Kim?" I asked. "How ya doing, my war angel?"

"I cannot believe it. We did it," Kim said.

"What?" I asked. I wasn't sure what she was talking about.

"We did it," she repeated.

The line was silent for a couple of moments, as I tried to figure out what she meant.

"What happened?"

"We did it," she said more emphatically. "You don't know?"

Shawn jumped in. "She doesn't know. You're telling her the news."

"Oh my gosh, Alice," Kim said. "You're out."

I screamed and began crying. I couldn't even respond. "I'm so sorry, I thought you knew," Kim continued. "The president just called me. He told me that you were out. He signed the papers, it's been released to the press. Everything."

I was screaming and crying and thanking God—a complete state of praise. I started jumping around. I have no idea how high, but I felt like my feet weren't touching the ground. I felt light, like a weight had been lifted off my shoulders and no longer held me in place. I felt like I could've jumped so high I could've touched the ceiling.

◇◇◇◇◇◇◇◇◇◇

For my family, the morning of June 6, 2018, was just another day of waiting, though the anticipation had grown more intense because of all the media rumors swirling over my release. The news anchors had been continually speculating on President Trump's visit with Kim, so my entire family was up early—each in their different homes and towns—magnetically drawn to the news. No one knew what to expect, but they wanted to absorb every syllable of hope.

They'd been on an emotional roller coaster for the past almost twenty-two years. How many times had the family phone tree buzzed with the hopeful phrase "I think this could be it"? I did not want my family to go through another agonizing defeat of a hopeful expectation.

Here's what the members of my family were doing when they received the call:

Tretessa (Daughter)

My oldest daughter was up early.

She had several calls, texts, and messages through her Facebook account requesting interviews because of all the press. That morning, she was about to do a live interview on MSNBC from CoverEDGE, a local studio in Phoenix, Arizona.

She was sitting in the makeup chair in the studio, as the makeup artist chatted about the possibility of her mother's release. "I'm rooting for your mama," she said as she applied a thin line of black eyeliner to the bottom of Tretessa's eye.

"I'm tentatively excited," Tretessa replied.

After she got her makeup on, she was called into the studio and mic'd up. She could hear a lot of background chatter in the MSNBC studio and took a few deep breaths to prepare for another interview. The producer quickly chimed in and introduced herself.

"Just making sure you can hear me," she said. "Testing, one, two."

"Loud and clear."

Then she said, "I'm sure you already know your mother's paperwork is on Trump's desk for him to sign."

"What?" Tretessa said. "No I didn't know that!" Before she could gather her composure, the producer said, "We are live in five, four, three . . ."

Tretessa did the interview, but it was a blur. After the interview ended, she picked up her purse to leave and felt her phone vibrate inside her bag. At 9:22 a.m., she received a text from Nick from *Nightly News with Lester Holt*. He'd had her number since she'd done an interview with them previously.

"Tretessa, CNN is reporting that the president has pardoned your mother. I'm so happy for you. I'm sure you are overwhelmed, but I just wanted to reach out and say congratulations and I am so glad your family will be complete."

Her mind went blank and body relaxed like it hadn't in nearly twenty-two years. How did the media find out before the family? Then Jennifer Turner called her, just seconds later, as she was about to walk out to the parking lot from the studio.

"Is it really true?" she asked. She just needed to hear it from someone on our legal team.

"Yes!" Jennifer responded. Tretessa was so giddy with joy that she wasn't even certain her responses were coherent. She must've told the makeup artist the good news, because the artist asked Tretessa if she was going to be able to drive or if she needed someone to walk her to the car. Tretessa could've floated to her car at that point.

Tretessa called Catina in the studio parking lot, and after a few shouts of joy, they talked excitedly as Tretessa drove to work. Tretessa had promised that if President Trump granted me clemency, she was going to change her Facebook profile picture to a photo of him. She told Catina that she was going to do just that.

"I'm so grateful that I probably would've named my twins

Kimberly and Donald if they weren't already born!" she said. After about forty minutes, Tretessa looked up and realized she had no idea where she was.

"Catina, I'm going to have to call you back," she said, grinning from ear to ear.

Charles (Son)

Charles hadn't been the type of guy who wanted to be in front of the cameras. His son Justin, the firstborn grandson, had done many more interviews than his dad. Charles drove Justin around to meet the various members of the media so frequently that the reporters often mistook him for a hired driver.

On that morning, Charles was at Justin's house, watching him prepare to do an interview with MIC. After Justin was finished being mic'd up, he walked to the kitchen. Charles heard the reporters talking about a message they had just gotten from their headquarters.

"Should we tell them now or later?" he overheard them ask each other.

Kendall came over and showed him the headline. His first thought was, *I hope this isn't fake.* Then he thought, *Maybe someone printed it wrong.*

He looked at it, then back at Kendall. "Are you sure that's right?"

He showed Justin.

Then he asked again. "Are you sure?"

Bryant (Son)

Bryant was working at his job loading trucks at Hobby Lobby that day. It also happened to be the first day he told his coworkers that his mother was incarcerated and that Kim Kardashian West was championing her case. Initially, his claim was met with skepticism.

"Are you for real?" they asked.

He was not allowed to talk on the phone at work, so he was surprised and worried when he checked his phone and saw that he'd missed forty-nine calls. He figured something awful had happened. Jason, his best friend since high school, was his last missed call. He called him back immediately.

"Man, where have you been?" Jason asked excitedly.

"At work—what's going on?" Bryant's stomach tightened.

"Your mama is free!"

"What?"

"It's been all over the news!"

Bryant told his supervisor and she let him leave. He practically sprinted home, which was about a mile away.

When he arrived, NBC was there, interviewing Tretessa.

Catina (Daughter)

Tretessa called Catina and broke the news.

"Turn on the television," she said. Catina ran to the television and found CNN, which was broadcasting photos of her mom, President Trump, and Kim Kardashian. That was a good sign that this was true. Catina talked to Tretessa until she got lost on her way to work. Then she called Jennifer.

"She got clemency!" Jennifer screamed through her tears. This caused Catina to scream out to tell her kids, Shelby and Kashea. Even though Tretessa had broken the news, CNN had echoed it, and Jennifer had confirmed it, she still had to remind herself it was real.

"Oh my God, it's true! Oh my God! Oh my God!" she said while galloping around the house.

Catina made sure her brother Charles, her aunts, and her uncle knew. When she got the chance to talk to me with my lawyers on the phone, she was thrilled to hear she could come pick me up immediately. She rushed around preparing to leave, but she kept going from room to room, forgetting what she'd come into each room for.

Julius (Brother)

After I told Julius that Kim was going to go to the White House, he decided to travel to Texas to visit friends and relatives. He wanted to believe that my release would happen soon, but he didn't want to get his hopes up. He planned on being gone for a five-day trip. But about halfway through the trip, his phone rang and rang. People were asking him when I was going to be released. The news coverage had been everywhere. Every time, he told them that nothing had been decided yet. After being gone about three days, he began getting restless. He said he felt like God was about to do something, so he got in the car and made it back to Memphis in record time.

The next morning, he got the call. Catina could barely get the words out. "Mama is free!"

Thelma (Sister)

Thelma was at a meeting in the Washington, DC, area when her phone vibrated. When she glanced at her phone, she saw that she had missed a call and text from Dolores. This was unusual, but the last few weeks had been filled with tense moments. When she called Dolores back, she heard the news and started to cry. She was overjoyed, but sad that she couldn't jump on the caravan that would be coming from Memphis.

Patricia (Sister)

Patricia awoke hours before her usual time. She set up her workstation right in front of the television. She kept the remote close so that she could switch channels quickly, since all the major news channels were covering the possibility of my clemency.

Her phone rang.

When she picked it up, she heard Catina's voice. Catina was talking so loudly and quickly that Patricia didn't understand what Catina was trying to say when she received the call . . . the one she'd prayed about every single day since I'd been in prison. She ran, cried, and praised God all at the same time.

Because Patricia lived in Jackson, Mississippi, she knew she needed to get to the family to be in the caravan. For years, they had planned to all drive to get me together. When Catina called her back, she figured she'd get instructions on my release. Would it be a day? A week? A month?

Catina had to repeat herself before Patricia understood. "It's immediate," she said. "We can go get her now!"

There was no time to caravan. She and her daughter Jasmine packed and headed straight to Aliceville within thirty minutes of receiving the call. About halfway to Aliceville, Jasmine asked, "Did anyone get Aunt Marie some clothes?"

Dolores (Sister)

Over the years, Dolores had made a vow to keep her car gassed up just in case she got "the call." She wanted to be ready to pick me up at the drop of a hat, so she never let her car get below half a tank. On that particular morning, she was headed to the service station to make sure that her car was filled.

When she got the call from Catina, it was as if she went into a rejoicing trance. She drove around and around and around, screaming and thanking God. She was so overjoyed that, after years of keeping her gas tank filled to the brim for this very moment, she returned home without getting any.

Coria (Sister)

That morning, Coria had gotten up and flipped on the television in the bedroom while she made the bed. No matter how many buttons she pushed on the remote, the television remained black. She quickened her pace to complete the bed when Dolores called, excitement in her voice.

"It looks like they are going to sign it!" she said.

Coria started getting nervous. They'd been down that road before. Then her phone rang again. This time it was Catina, and Coria started crying and hollering. Her husband, Samuel, rushed into the bedroom.

"What's wrong?" he asked. "I heard wailing."

Through muffled tears, she was able to give him the news. They told their family to come over and they'd all load up into the RV, but it wasn't registering. Instead, they decided to ride with Dolores in her SUV. (Dolores said she'd be right over, but she had to go get more gas.) Samuel decided to stay at the house because the MIC film crew had gone directly to their home after the announcement and started filming.

MIC interviewed Julius when he arrived, and then Coria. Their cat, Smokey, kept running up to Coria and jumping up as if she were trying her best to be seen. Coria stomped the ground so Smokey would settle down. She definitely didn't want MIC to start filming that cat. Then they loaded up the SUV.

Their road trip was filled with phone calls and excited chatter. Since they realized that Thelma was upset about not being able to caravan, they FaceTimed her to give her updates.

When Patricia called on her trip from Jackson, they all realized that I didn't have any nice clothes. They told her to drive to the closest mall. There, Patricia broke several of her shopping rules: she skipped the clearance rack and didn't even look for a coupon.

She scooped up several outfits without even checking the prices.

◇◇◇◇◇◇◇◇◇◇

It had happened.

I walked out of that room and could hear cheering, clapping, and my name being shouted in the hallway—women celebrating the announcement on both sides, units B3 and B4. Some of them had their faces pressed against the glass, and I could see so many tears, tears, and more tears. A staff member opened the B4 side so that I could say goodbye to my friends, and we were all crying and hugging. I could hear cries of "Don't forget us, Miss Alice!" The guards signaled that I needed to leave and go back to my unit.

When I walked back to my door, the same scene was repeated— so much love and genuine joy.

I heard my name being shouted from downstairs. "Miss Alice, *please* come out!" I walked downstairs and made my way outside to a sea of women, hugging, crying, and praising God. It looked like the dorms had emptied themselves out, and I was being swarmed by these beautiful women who had become my prison family. My heart swelled and was bursting with so many emotions.

"Clear the yard!" I heard over the intercom. "Return to your units."

My friend Fifty (who was really named Barbara Turner) was still holding my hand so tightly that she came up to my unit with me. I asked the staff for permission for her to stay a little longer. Fifty was also a lifer, like me, and a very gifted artist. We had worked on every play and project together since I'd arrived at Aliceville. Then I asked if two friends could come over—Cristie and Casiana—and my friends Dorothy, Jennifer, and Chola were standing at the door crying. Friends from other countries were swarming my door with well wishes in their native tongues. As I hurried to change clothes and try to give friends mementos, my counselor, Ms. Hullet, came to the door and told me to hurry up.

"Take whatever you want!" I said to my friends. "Give some to the needy! I need to try and curl my hair!" My friends went into action, starting to curl and pin my hair.

Then I heard, "Alice Marie Johnson, report to R&D with all of your property." R&D was shorthand for "Receiving and Discharge," where prisoners are first received and later discharged when their time is up.

A big cheer went up from all over the prison.

Case manager Mr. Holler, Ms. Hullet, Fifty, and Casiana walked with me out the door. As I was walking down the stairs, I heard what sounded like the rumblings of an earthquake. As I started my walk to R&D, everywhere I looked, women were pressed against the windows and hitting the bars, screaming my name and crying. The sound seemed to get louder and louder with each step I took, until the crescendo sounded like a million fans cheering in a football stadium. It was surround sound on steroids.

All for me.

I paused, looked around, and waved goodbye. Then I clutched

my heart and made the motion of pulling my heart out of my chest and throwing it to them. The cheer that went up was deafening. I continued my walk to R&D. When I arrived, Ms. Jenkins and Ms. Howard were waiting on me. Within the hour, I would receive two papers: one saying "Release Date: Unknown," the second one saying "Time Served: June 6, 2018."

Staff members were coming to the R&D to say goodbye, including my former counselor, Mr. Flowers, a die-hard Auburn fan. Chaplain Floyd came to pray for me for the last time in prison. She had been an anchor for me in the heartbreak of my clemency denial. I wished I could've thanked all the staff members who were so kind to me, but the list would be too long. Finally, the moment I had dreamed about for over two decades: I walked out the door and into freedom.

Only one car was allowed to come onto the premises to pick me up. My son Charles was the driver of the rented van. In the van was also Catina, Julius, my granddaughters Shelby and Kashea, my great-grandson D'Angelo, and my new daughter-in-law Shontoria. I had never physically hugged her, since my son and she had met and married while I was in prison.

The rest of my family members were told to park and wait across the road from the prison. As we exited the parking lot, I passed the camp where approximately 250 minimum-security women were housed. As I neared the camp, another scene unfolded: every woman and every staff member was standing outside. Some were cheering, some were clapping, some were rejoicing, and others were crying. It was just like the scene I had just left. They were shouting, "We love you, Miss Alice. Don't forget us!"

My family looked on in amazement.

As I neared the spot where the rest of my family was waiting, I saw TV satellites and news reporters from every media outlet in America. Then I saw my family. Before the van could come to a stop, I jumped out. I ran—it felt like I flew—into the arms of my beloved family. My sister Dolores met me with roses. Out of a heart overflowing with gratitude, I thanked my Lord and Savior Jesus Christ, President Donald John Trump, Kim, my family, and all the ones who'd fought for me.

Chapter 15

⁓

"Take me home."

I had given interviews to the press at the foot of the prison compound, where I talked emotionally about my freedom. When that was over, it was finally time to go.

I began the long journey home.

Catina had to tell me which car was hers—the blue one—and I climbed in while the cameras rolled. I waved and gestured with my hands, because it was the first time I'd been in a vehicle without shackles in over two decades. None of those cutting leg irons either.

Catina drove, and my granddaughters talked in the back seat. I kept pausing as I listened to the GPS system electronically instruct her how to get home from the prison—a big upgrade from paper maps, but also a little distracting. I'd never heard anything like that before. The car beeped and dinged and seemed to talk back in a way I'd never seen. I soon learned no one gives directions, they give addresses.

On the way home, the media called and I gave interviews. I talked to Anderson Cooper on CNN live, while my daughter Tretessa was also on via satellite. She hadn't been able to come to my release all the way from Arizona on such short notice, but she was there in spirit. I saw her in the faces of my other family members. I told Anderson that I would not disappoint America. So many people had put their trust in me. It was almost like there was a big buildup of anticipation between the time that Kim told people about my plight and the moment she met with President Trump. Many people told me they were praying for me—individually and entire churches.

"I want to tell President Trump that you will not regret giving me this second chance on life," I told Anderson Cooper. "I will not disappoint the American public, who had so much faith in me." While I was talking, my eighteen-month-old great-grandson babbled in the background, but I loved that. The sound of children. The sound of family. That's what I wanted to be my soundtrack for the rest of my life.

When we neared my sister Coria's house, my pulse quickened as I saw cars lined up everywhere. We turned into the driveway of her spacious home, and I took a moment to thank God for my miracle. The rest of the caravan of family members who had traveled to Mississippi were pulling up in their cars too. As I alighted from the car, I could hear the sounds of laughter and excited voices. Someone opened the door of the house and yelled, "She's here!" I was met with shouts, screams, and so many tears. Everyone was trying to get near me and touch me at the same time. By this time, I was sobbing and looking at my family through a blur of tears. "I'm home! I'm home!" I just kept repeating. There was not a dry eye in the room, including the journalists who were inside with my family.

The wonderful aroma of food penetrated my senses. I looked around, and the only word I can use to describe the feast before me was INCREDIBLE. In just three hours, my nieces and nephews had come together to cook a scrumptious meal that included fried chicken, fish, spaghetti and meatballs, coleslaw, cobblers, cakes, pecan pies, fresh vegetables, and so much more good southern food. I looked around and saw the faces of so many relatives I didn't recognize and some I'd never met. But I knew they were family because of the resemblance to everyone else. There were also gathered inside the house friends who'd come as soon as they discovered that I was going to be at Coria's.

After we finished eating, my nieces Sherri and Shelia started singing what had become a theme song for my family as they fought and prayed for me: Mary Mary's "Can't Give Up Now." We all joined in and sang the chorus with them. More tears of thanksgiving flowed. Finally it was time to leave. My brother, Julius, and I had planned for years that when I got out of prison I would stay with him as long as I wanted to. My family and friends brought clothing over so that I would have extra changes of clothes. My sister Coria packed a necessities bag for me—underwear, toiletries, and pajamas. I was all set for my first night outside prison.

When I arrived at Julius's house, he showed me around. Without being invited to, I opened his refrigerator and looked inside. That really excited me, to be able to open that door. The last time I'd opened a refrigerator door in a house was October 31, 1996.

Julius showed me to my room, and I saw a sight that made me freeze in my tracks—a king-size bed. After I finished my shower and put my pajamas on, I made sure my brother wasn't looking. Then I dived onto the bed and made a snow angel on top of it. I rolled around and laughed and kicked my legs and bounced up and down like a kid. No more bunk beds!

The next morning, I went on a marathon of interviews and television appearances. (The last one was at two a.m. live on *Good Morning Britain.*) One thing that several reporters asked me about was what I was looking forward to getting now that I was out of prison.

"I want one of those smartphones that everyone has," I replied. Now that I was out of prison, I noticed that everywhere I looked people were walking around talking on the phone and texting. Some were FaceTiming. One of my favorite television shows growing up was *The Jetsons.* They had phones where you could see the person you were talking to. I thought at the time that this was some futuristic sci-fi stuff, not knowing that one day I'd be walking around and be able to see people on the phone, too. When I did get a smartphone, I was really confused about how to use it. I remarked, "Now that I have a smartphone, I realize I'm the dummy!" My grandson agreed to give me a tutorial.

Kim generously made accommodations for my daughter Tretessa and her three-month-old twins—Amira Charlotte and Aiden Charles (dubbed the grandtwins) and my son Bryant to spend some time with me. They flew in from Arizona to Memphis, arriving on June 11, and were treated like royalty.

Finally, the date was set for me to meet Kim Kardashian West in person for the first time. *Keeping Up with the Kardashians*, the *Today* show, and MIC filming crews arrived early on Wednesday, June 13, to capture our first meeting. It was one week since I'd been released when Kim landed in a private jet in Memphis and headed across the Tennessee–Mississippi border.

Let me tell you, the small town of Southaven was not used to this level of excitement. At around ten o'clock, satellite trucks arrived at Coria's house. Local reporters also arrived, setting up at the end of the driveway, their long camera lenses focused on the house every second. Then, as news drifted through the town that Kim was coming, people slowly began driving by, hoping to catch a glimpse of her. Neighbors joined the reporters waiting across the street. They were all excited when they saw the caravan coming down the two-lane road.

I interviewed with Hoda Kotb of the *Today* show, first by myself before Kim arrived, and told her about a picture that I had of Kim and Kanye from when they were in high school. I'd torn it from a magazine and placed it in my Bible so I could pray for them every day.

One of the show's producers asked me if I still had that picture in my Bible. "Yes, but my Bible is at my brother's house," I said.

"Do you think someone could go get it?" he asked. "Do you remember where you last had it, so they could grab it?"

Of course I knew where my Bible was located. I'd be more likely to misplace my toothbrush than my Bible. The producers took Julius to his house and I told him where my Bible was. But when he grabbed it, he flipped through the pages and said, "I didn't see the picture in there."

"It's there," I said, knowing that the pages were so thin that sometimes it's hard to find your place. "Just come on back and bring it."

Kim arrived at my sister's around one p.m. The reporters documented every second. Even though the media was set up at the end of my sister's long driveway, their audio equipment would pick up every sound. Along with my big family, three of my attorneys were there: Mike Scholl, the local attorney in Memphis; Jennifer Turner (whom I'd met in person for the first time the night before); and Brittany Barnett, whom I had seen in prison face-to-face in Carswell when she was a law student. Hoda would be interviewing Kim and me after our reunion. (By the way, I simply love Hoda. She had us laughing and singing so much, and she blended right in with my family.)

When Kim rang the doorbell, I answered it and we both screamed then hugged each other so tightly. Finally I was meeting the woman who went to war to save my life. Meeting Kim did not feel like I was meeting a celebrity; it felt like I was meeting a friend. Walking in right behind Kim was my lead attorney, Shawn Holley. I didn't greet Shawn as warmly, because I didn't recognize her. Her hair was in a ponytail. She looked so young, I thought she was Kim's assistant! I was expecting her to look like an older woman to match all her accomplishments.

I can't tell you what it was like to meet this woman who had saved my life in person. We laughed, cried, reminisced, and talked about southern cooking. I told her I'd love to cook for her one day, and she agreed to let me do just that. Kim also showed me what Snapchat looked like, and she put funny ears and noses on pictures of both of us—which I loved seeing.

Another exciting moment was when Kim called Kanye and passed me the phone.

"Hi, Kanye. I'm sitting here in front of your beautiful wife. I want you to know that the people here in Memphis love you," I said. "This is something that gives not only prisoners hope, but America hope. You played a big role in this." I know Kanye had opened the door for my release through his support of President Trump.

When Kim and I interviewed with Hoda jointly, Hoda asked me to tell Kim about how I prayed for her and Kanye. I knew the photo would be located at Isaiah 54:17. When Hoda handed me my Bible, I turned right to it. I explained that I had been praying protection around them. "No weapon formed against Kim and Kanye shall prosper. And every tongue which rises against them in judgment, they shall condemn it." They better not mess with Kim, not even with their tongue.

What a day it was! It was one that will live in my heart forever. But it wouldn't be the last time I would see Kim in person. In October, we would both be invited to the Google offices in Mountain View, California, for a fireside chat on criminal justice reform with Malika Saada Saar.

Later, in November, I was invited to Los Angeles—to the city Kim and Kanye call home—with my sisters Patricia and Dolores. I sent a list of ingredients in advance, so I could show Kim how to cook biscuits from scratch, the easy way. We also made beef and gravy, fried chicken, cream potatoes, baked macaroni, collard greens, and much more. I got to meet and eat dinner with Kanye, Kim's sisters, and her mother and her children. Even some of her extended family members—nieces and nephews—came to meet me. They were so kind, and just regular people. They reminded me so much of how close my family is. While we chatted, I noticed that Kris was crying at the table. I think she was thinking of what it would've been like to be locked up and separated from her family.

Although people from around the world saw me running across the street on June 6, 2018, what they don't know is that I've been running ever since, fighting for those I left behind. I have had the opportunity to speak on numerous platforms and appear with some of the greatest thought leaders of the day.

Never in my wildest dreams would I have imagined that I would be honored at the United Nations for fighting for the rights of women and using my voice to magnify their issues while I was in prison. I was selected as one of four women from around the world to be honored on International Women's Day, March 8, at the United Nations. We were the first to receive the Women's Rights Defender designation, and I was the only one from North America.

Every year, a clip is made of the most searched-for people and topics of the year. I was included in the "Google Year in Search 2018." As news of President Trump granting me clemency at the request of Kim Kardashian West broke, people wanted to find out more about me.

President Donald Trump continues to talk about the day I

was released from prison and how it made him feel. He loved seeing my family after over two decades of separation reunite and celebrate. When the president signed the First Step Act into law on December 21, 2018, he spoke of me. To have touched the heart of a president leaves me in awe.

I am very humbled by where this journey has taken me. My story is more than a story of a woman given a life sentence and then a second chance at life. It is more than a story of hope just for prisoners. It is a story of hope for all people. Everyone has experienced the death of something or someone.

The loss of a dream, of health, of a relationship, and maybe even of freedom. Whatever the loss, we all have this in common: we suffered. But after life as you may have known it has come to an end—either expected or unexpected—there is still hope for a future that is not determined by your position or your condition in life. No matter the circumstances, your past and present do not have to be your future, as long as you believe.

Epilogue

It felt good to be free, but my friends behind bars were always on my mind.

Because of that, I tried to use my platform to draw attention to the First Step Act, a bipartisan bill aimed at criminal justice reform that had been working its way through Congress. Among other things, this act would shorten mandatory minimum sentences and reduce the number of nonviolent drug offenders who get mandatory sentencing. Though it's hard to get things done in Washington, DC, I hoped that one day the women I'd met in prison might experience the freedom I now enjoyed. Considering the divisive nature of politics, the First Step Act was far from a sure thing, but one advantage was that people from both sides were in support of it. Apparently criminal justice reform was an issue that brought people together.

This was true in politics and in person. One day I was sitting at home when my phone rang. Kim and Khloe were on the phone, telling me about an event that was going to take place in

West Hollywood in a couple of weeks. *Variety* and *Rolling Stone* were cohosting their first-ever Criminal Justice Reform Summit in Los Angeles, and Kim was asked to speak, along with CNN host and activist Van Jones and hip-hop artist Meek Mill.

"Will you come with me?" Kim asked.

I wouldn't miss it for the world.

I traveled to Los Angeles on November 12, and two days later, the day of the event, I woke up and checked my email. The White House had requested my presence for an important announcement: the president was going to endorse the criminal justice reform bill.

Tears began to stream down my face. It was really happening.

Since I was on the West Coast, I wasn't able to find a flight on such short notice to make it to the White House by the time of the announcement. I was so disappointed—I doubted I'd have another opportunity to celebrate the cause I'd so heavily championed with the president of the United States. As I searched for a flight from Los Angeles to Washington, DC, I couldn't help but think of how much my life had changed from when I was locked up for so many years.

My sisters Dolores and Patricia and I got ready for the Criminal Justice Reform Summit and were taken to the event at the Jeremy Hotel. There, we waited in a room for the event to begin. When Van Jones and Kim arrived, I greeted them with a hug.

"President Trump is making an announcement!" someone said. Activist Louis Reed held his phone out and everyone gathered around to try to listen, including Van, Kim, myself, and other activists.

"Today, I'm thrilled to announce my support for this bipartisan bill that will make our communities safer and give former inmates a second chance at life after they have served their time." It was such a powerful moment, one that lessened my sorrow over not being at the White House. Everyone was so excited, and tears began to roll down my face. Then, to my surprise, I heard my name.

"I'll give an example of Miss Alice Johnson, who served twenty-one years," President Trump said. "I'll never forget the scene of her coming out of prison . . . and greeting her family and everybody was crying. Her sons, her grandsons—everybody was crying and hugging and holding each other. It was a beautiful thing to see."

I didn't get to exactly hear everything, because of the excitement and emotions of the group. Plus, it was time for Kim and Van to take the stage. My sisters and I settled into our seats at a front table and were eager to hear the discussion on such a historic day.

Van began by describing Kim as "one of the most effective and impactful criminal justice advocates." Then, he told the room what we'd just heard. "While we are sitting here," he said, "President Donald Trump is in the Roosevelt Room with a bunch of senators, a bunch of our friends, a bunch of TV cameras, announcing that he is going to support the First Step Act."

People erupted into applause and tears. This was the first meaningful criminal justice reform in decades.

Van marveled about how enthusiastically President Trump had gotten behind prison reform, and even mentioned that President

Trump loved to talk about me. "By the way, Miss Alice Johnson is here," he said, pointing to me. He asked the room to give me a round of applause. I stood and waved to the room, full of joy—not because I was being recognized, but because my friends languishing in the system would finally have a chance at freedom.

On December 20, the House overwhelmingly voted in support of the First Step Act. The next day, President Trump made it official by signing the bipartisan criminal justice bill. I was absolutely glued to the television that day, watching every second of the coverage. All over Twitter, my fellow activists were celebrating. I had a very personal reason for my joy: I knew many of the dear friends I'd made in prison finally had a chance of being released. Over the course of the next few months, that's exactly what happened.

Thankfully, the First Step announcement was not the only chance I had of going to the White House.

◇◇◇◇◇◇◇◇◇◇

On Friday, February 1, 2019, I was at a family gathering in Memphis, Tennessee. At 8:18 p.m., a text message appeared on my phone. I didn't recognize the 202 area code, but the message made my heart thud. A woman named Madeleine with President Trump's office wanted me to give her a call.

Hurriedly, I went to a private area and called her. Madeleine told me the White House was extending an invitation to me to attend the State of the Union address on February 6 in Washington, DC. President Trump had personally requested my presence at this event.

Since coming home from prison, I rarely traveled alone. My sisters Dolores and Patricia usually accompany me. So the White House made arrangements for all three of us to travel together and to arrive in the nation's capital on Monday, February 5.

After landing, we checked into our hotel rooms, but when I finally retired for the night, sleep didn't come easily. Throughout the night I couldn't help but reflect upon my journey from incarceration into freedom. If only I had known the plans of God all along for my future, it would have saved me a lot of tears and heartache. But that's not how God or faith operates. All the seemingly unanswered prayers didn't fall on deaf ears. I now know He was listening and answered them in His own way. God had the perfect timing for my miracle to take place.

When I awoke the next morning, I'd gotten at least a few hours of sleep. The day had finally arrived when I'd shake the hand of the man who signed the papers that set me free and restored me to my family.

We arrived at the White House shortly after 12:30 p.m. and had to pass through various high-security checkpoints. After clearance, we received badges and were escorted into a waiting room where we met other invited guests and their families. I was only in that room a few minutes when Avi (Avraham) Berkowitz sought me out to tell me that Jared Kushner wanted to meet me. Avi and Cassidy Dumbauld had both worked tirelessly on my clemency paperwork for Jared, so I was very excited to meet them too. (All through the day I met White House staffers who told me how they had prayed and rooted for my release from prison. This really warmed my heart.) When Jared walked into the room, he gave me a big hug. I'd spoken to him only a few times after my release, but he instantly put me at ease.

I had two cards in my purse. At Christmas, my daughter Tretessa made cards that featured a photo of me, two of my kids, and my grandtwins. Tretessa sent these out to everyone who had played a role in my freedom. But I had two remaining cards to give to the last people on the list, the ones I wanted to deliver by hand. One of the cards was for Jared and Ivanka. The other was for the president. I wanted them to see me restored. I wanted them to know they made Christmas with my family possible. I wanted to thank them, but how can you ever show someone who saved your life the amount of gratitude they deserve? These cards would have to do. I handed Jared and Ivanka their card but had to give the president's to a staffer to run through the proper channels. He hadn't arrived yet, but the room was electric as we waited for him.

Then the moment came. All the other State of the Union guests and their families were lined up to meet President Donald John Trump. My heart raced as each guest and their family were announced and ushered forward to meet the president and take a picture. When my turn came, before I could be announced, President Trump looked at me and said, "I know who this is. Alice Johnson." I quickly walked to him and shook his extended hand and said, "Thank you, Mr. President." I wanted to give him a big thank-you hug and say so much more; however, protocol and the line behind me would not allow for it. My sisters and I were positioned on both sides of President Trump and we all smiled for our official White House photo. I walked away, and then turned back toward the president and silently said, "Thank you."

We were then given a grand tour of the White House and I was in awe of the historic residence. After the tour, Vice President and Mrs. Pence hosted a reception for all of us. We took pictures with them and I was presented with a gift from Vice President Pence. Around 5:00 p.m. we were served a gourmet dinner in the White House. After dinner, we were sent to another waiting area to line up to meet First Lady Melania Trump.

While we were waiting in line, Ivanka entered the room. She looked at me and exclaimed, "Alice!" We hugged, talked, and laughed . . . our eyes were filled with tears. Ivanka pulled out her phone and took a selfie of us and said she was sending it to Kim Kardashian West.

Then I met the First Lady, Melania Trump, who greeted me with so much genuine warmth. We then posed for a picture. Before I left, I was presented with a gift, a beautiful gold coin emblazoned with the First Lady's insignia.

All the State of the Union invited guests were given new security badges and taken to a bus for transport to the House of Representatives' chambers. Our family members remained at the White House and were taken to a private room to watch the address together live on a large-screen television. My sisters later told me how all the families bonded in that room and how they shed some tears when they learned I'd spent over two decades behind bars separated from my family.

Our bus followed the First Lady's motorcade. I have never ridden in a vehicle on land that traveled that fast. Since all the streets were blocked and the roads were completely cleared, we didn't have to stop for any traffic lights. The ride of a lifetime.

I'll never forget seeing the United States Capitol building up close for the first time. The top is adorned with the bronze Statue of Freedom, a woman holding a sheathed sword in one hand, a wreath in her other, and the words *e pluribus unum* at her feet. How appropriate that this building, where laws are passed that shape the destiny of so many people, is watched over by a statue symbolizing liberty and unity.

When I alighted from the bus, I asked myself for the fiftieth time, "Why did I wear these high heels?" My feet were already aching, and I was just told the walk to our seats would entail climbing over eighty steps. Thankfully someone saw me walking sideways and asked if I would like to get on the elevator.

I was led to my assigned seat in the presidential guest box. Like Joseph in the Bible, God had elevated me—a prisoner—to become the invited guest of the highest-ranking official in the nation. As I looked around at our nation's leaders representing people all over America, my heart swelled with emotions too numerous to articulate. I felt so humbled to have a seat of honor among this prestigious assembly that included members of Congress and Supreme Court justices. Then, President Trump walked in and people applauded.

When he began his speech, I watched the faces in the crowd, most of whom I had only seen on television or in news articles. Suddenly, the president started to speak about me. "Last year, I heard through friends the story of Alice Johnson." I braced myself.

"She had a big impact on that prison population—and far beyond. Alice's story underscores the disparities and unfairness that can exist in criminal sentencing—and the need to remedy this total injustice." I pressed my shoulders against the back of my seat. I've never been one to cry easily, but the tears began to flow.

The president continued. "When I saw Alice's beautiful family greet her at the prison gates, hugging and kissing and crying and laughing, I knew I did something right," he said. "Alice, thank you for reminding us that we always have the power to shape our own destiny."

As people applauded, the president added, "She is a terrific woman. Terrific."

Alice Marie Johnson, who had been called "terrible," was just called "TERRIFIC" by the president of the United States of America.

I looked around and beheld the room filled with people from across the political divide giving me a standing ovation. One year ago, I stood in front of a guard for nightly prison count. Tonight, I stood in front of America for thunderous applause.

To God be the glory!

Acknowledgments

To my war angel, Kim Kardashian West—you are my gift from Heaven. You fought for me and never stopped fighting. Blessings to you and Kanye for your amazing support. Words can't express my debt to you, but I will pray for you in gratitude for the rest of my life.

A special thanks to President Donald John Trump. Thank you for believing in me and giving me a second chance. You restored me to my family. I'll spend the rest of my days trying to make you proud of your act of mercy. You won't regret it.

Thank you, Jared Kushner and Ivanka Trump. You joined in the fight for my freedom and your tenacity helped me gain the victory!

Thank you to my incredible attorneys whom Kim assembled— Shawn Holley, Jennifer Turner, Brittany Barnett, and Mike Scholl. Over the months that you joined forces to rescue me from prison, we developed a beautiful bond that will last forever. You are my own "Dream Team."

Marcia Shein, thank you for taking me on as a pro bono client to fight for my clemency during Clemency Project 2014. Though that ultimately didn't happen through that initiative, you helped begin the fight which ended in my walking out of those prison doors as a free woman.

Thank you to the Buried Alive Project. Your support upon my reentry was invaluable. The work you do is truly life-saving.

Thank you to Google and YouTube for using your technology to make a difference in my life and the world.

Thank you, Malika Saada Saar, for your advocacy and love. You've expanded my horizons by giving me many opportunities I'd never otherwise have.

Thank you to the ACLU—you were the first ones to give me a public platform with the article by Jennifer Turner, "A Living Death." That piece opened the eyes of many Americans to our plight.

This list wouldn't be complete without thanking the great people at MIC.com. Who could've predicted how viral that incredible video would go! Thanks especially to CEO Jake Horowitz, Kendall Ciesemier, Abu Zafar, Bruno Silva, and Stephen Valdivia for all of your work.

Thanks to Topeka Sam for seizing every opportunity to lift up my case. You have helped me and so many other women to hold on to our dignity while in prison.

Thank you, Amy Povah, for your "can do" attitude. I appreciate your tireless efforts to increase public awareness about my cause and for your encouragement to me in hard times.

Andrea James, I'm so thankful for your work and for the National Council of Incarcerated and Formerly Incarcerated Women and Girls.

Thanks also to Syrita Steib ("Pretty"), who fought for me. So proud of you.

Thanks to Nkechi Taifa for giving me platforms in and out of prison. I appreciate you for getting my children to the White House so they could fight for me.

Thanks, Mark Osler, for your support and for lifting up my name on national television for clemency.

Thank you, Van Jones and #cut50 staff for fighting so hard to change hearts and laws. You are making a difference.

Thanks to Mark Holden for putting me under your wing after I got out of prison. I'm so impressed by your dedication to fighting overcriminalization. You are on the front lines of making this world better for so many people.

Thank you, Evangelist Kene and Apostle Dr. Linda Holliday. You were with me in the early days and continued to fight for me to come home. You helped nurture me spiritually and gave me an invaluable ministry platform.

Thanks, Roach Brown, for broadcasting the first Clemency and Criminal Justice Radiothon. You got my voice out to the public in a big way.

Thanks, attorney Eddye Lane for what you did for me and for being a close family friend. You fought for me and helped in my time of need.

Thank you, attorney Danica Mathes, for the hard work you

did in making sure I could navigate through the numerous rounds of paperwork necessary to make sound decisions.

To the staff at FCI Dublin, FMC Carswell, and FCI Aliceville, I appreciate so many kindnesses, and thank you for giving me opportunities to use my gifts in prison. A special thank-you to Warden Washington-Aducci and Mr. Aubrey Collins, who wrote letters on my behalf.

Thank you, prison chaplains, for my spiritual growth during tough times. You helped me find strength even in prison, which was a balm for my soul.

Thank you, TBN and Daystar, for your inspirational programming throughout the years.

Thank you, Edward Stanton III, former US Attorney for the Western District of Tennessee. You took the time to listen to my family and wrote a letter in support of my clemency.

Thank you to the Olive Branch High School class of 1973 and Eastside Elementary, Junior High, and Senior High School.

I especially appreciate the teachers at Eastside High School, who helped instill in me a sense of pride in who I am.

Congressman Bennie Thompson, Steve Cohen, and Marc Veasey—thank you for the letters you wrote on my behalf for clemency (and to all of the others who did as well, even if they didn't know me!).

Thank you, Jonathan Perri, for working so hard on my behalf, and all of the more than 270,000 of you who supported and signed my petition on Change.org.

Thank you to the NAACP, and especially to T. L. Plunkett,

president of the DeSoto County Mississippi chapter, for your advocacy.

Thank you to former Deputy Sheriff Randy Wade for joining my family in fighting to bring me home.

A special thank-you to the all-women crew at Novus Select who filmed me for the United Nations: director Megan Sullivan; producer Thea Hardy; director of photography, VR, Jenn Duong; director of photography, traditional, Eve Cohen; drone operator and sound Danielle de Leon; and photographer Melissa Lyttle. You made work fun.

Thank you to Prison Fellowship for the seminars conducted while I was in prison. Thank you to the Potter's House of Dallas, Texas, for the Bible Studies. Thanks, Pickens County Baptist Association, a fantastic community for me in Aliceville. All of these organization, along with other ministries that came into the prison, really lived up to the Biblical call: I was in prison and you visited me.

To the women I met in prison who shared the journey with me, thank you so much! All of you are tattooed on my heart.

Thank you to my family in the faith community for your many prayers and support. I know what prayer can do!

Thank you to ALL of the advocates and activists who have fought so long and hard for criminal justice reform. You are the unsung heroes of the movement. May your rewards be great in this life and the one to come. Amen.

I need to really thank the amazing folks who made this book happen. This includes the fabulous Mel Berger, David Hines, Lance Klein, and Elizabeth Wachtel. You are the absolute best.

I so appreciate the people at HarperCollins. Thanks to president and publisher Jonathan Burnham and senior vice president and publisher Doug Jones for giving me this opportunity. Lisa Sharkey, thank you for pursuing me and for believing in my story and in this book. I so enjoyed getting to know Matt Harper, whose edits helped me really convey my thoughts in a more compelling way. Thanks to Anna Montague for your help with all of the photos. Thanks to Maddie Pillari, to Robin Bilardello (who created a great cover), to Christine Choe (who helped with marketing), and to Rachel Elinsky and Tina Andreadis (for the publicity). What an honor to have my name on the cover of a book after all these years of writing stories, plays, and musicals while I was in prison. You made my dream come true.

I found in Nancy French the perfect match for this literary collaboration. Thank you, beautiful lady, for capturing my voice and working with me like a hand in a glove. We have experienced the miraculous over and over while working on this book. A true Divine Connection!

A big thank-you and a virtual hug to all of my close friends, especially Sharanda Jones. Your friendship and affection helped me make it through.

Mere words are not enough to express my deep appreciation for my family. You are very important to me.

I love all of my children: Tretessa, Catina, Charles, Bryant, and Cory (Coco).

Thanks to Tretessa, Catina, Charles, and Bryant for supporting one another and enduring more than two decades without me. Thank you for loving each other and staying together as family in the tragic aftermath of Cory's death and in my absence.

To my grandchildren—Justin, Shelby, Kashea, Christopher, Amira, and Aiden—and great-grandchildren—D'Angelo and Alana. Grandma/GG is home NOW—to make wonderful and fun memories with you!

Thank you to my incredible siblings: Lena, Celestine, Coria, Thelma, Julius, Patricia, Ruby, and Dolores. Each of you are the best anyone could wish for. Also, thanks to my brothers-in-law, who enriched our family by loving my sisters: Thomas, Walter, Samuel, Jeffery, Vaughn, and Reginald.

Thank you to my wonderful nieces, nephews, cousins, and aunt, I will never forget your prayers, support, and how you showered me with love.

And most of all, I thank my Lord and Savior Jesus Christ who has sustained me throughout my life. He alone is my HOPE.